P9-APW-688

THE IMPORTANCE OF

Amelia Earhart

These and other titles are included in The Importance Of
biography series:

Alexander the Great	Harry Houdini
Muhammad Ali	Thomas Jefferson
Louis Armstrong	Chief Joseph
Clara Barton	Malcolm X
Napoleon Bonaparte	Margaret Mead
Rachel Carson	Michelangelo
Charlie Chaplin	Wolfgang Amadeus Mozart
Winston Churchill	Sir Isaac Newton
Cleopatra	Richard M. Nixon
Christopher Columbus	Georgia O'Keeffe
Marie Curie	Louis Pasteur
Amelia Earhart	Pablo Picasso
Thomas Edison	Jackie Robinson
Albert Einstein	Anwar Sadat
Dian Fossey	Margaret Sanger
Benjamin Franklin	John Steinbeck
Galileo Galilei	Jim Thorpe
Martha Graham	Mark Twain
Stephen Hawking	H. G. Wells
Jim Henson	

THE IMPORTANCE OF

Amelia Earhart

by
Eileen Morey

B
EARHART

Lucent Books, P.O. Box 289011, San Diego, CA 92198-9011

VRW P6 J4

Library of Congress Cataloging-in-Publication Data

Morey, Eileen, 1923–
    Amelia Earhart / by Eileen Morey.
        p.   cm.—(The Importance of)
    Includes bibliographical references (p.   ) and index.
    ISBN 1-56006-065-4 (alk. paper)
    1. Earhart, Amelia, 1897–1937—Juvenile literature.
2. Women air pilots—United States—Biography—Juvenile
literature. [1. Earhart, Amelia, 1897–1937. 2. Air pilots.
3. Women—Biography.]   I. Title. II. Series.
TL540.E3M65   1995
629.13'092—dc20   94-556
[B]   CIP
                                             AC

Copyright 1995 by Lucent Books, Inc., P.O. Box 289011,
San Diego, California, 92198-9011

Printed in the U.S.A.

No part of this book may be reproduced or used in any other
form or by any other means, electrical, mechanical, or other-
wise, including, but not limited to, photocopy, recording, or
any information storage and retrieval system, without prior
written permission from the publisher.

Contents

Foreword

THE IMPORTANCE OF biography series deals with individuals who have made a unique contribution to history. The editors of the series have deliberately chosen to cast a wide net and include people from all fields of endeavor. Individuals from politics, music, art, literature, philosophy, science, sports, and religion are all represented. In addition, the editors did not restrict the series to individuals whose accomplishments have helped change the course of history. Of necessity, this criterion would have eliminated many whose contribution was great, though limited. Charles Darwin, for example, was responsible for radically altering the scientific view of the natural history of the world. His achievements continue to impact the study of science today. Others, such as Chief Joseph of the Nez Percé, played a pivotal role in the history of their own people. While Joseph's influence does not extend much beyond the Nez Percé, his nonviolent resistance to white expansion and his continuing role in protecting his tribe and his homeland remain an inspiration to all.

These biographies are more than factual chronicles. Each volume attempts to emphasize an individual's contributions both in his or her own time and for posterity. For example, the voyages of Christopher Columbus opened the way to European colonization of the New World. Unquestionably, his encounter with the New World brought monumental changes to both Europe and the Americas in his day. Today, however, the broader impact of Columbus's voyages is being critically scrutinized. *Christopher Columbus,* as well as every biography in The Importance Of series, includes and evaluates the most recent scholarship available on each subject.

Each author includes a wide variety of primary and secondary source quotations to document and substantiate his or her work. All quotes are footnoted to show readers exactly how and where biographers derive their information, as well as to provide stepping stones to further research. These quotations enliven the text by giving readers eyewitness views of the life and times of each individual covered in The Importance Of series.

Finally, each volume is enhanced by photographs, bibliographies, chronologies, and comprehensive indexes. For both the casual reader and the student engaged in research, The Importance Of biographies will be a fascinating adventure into the lives of people who have helped shape humanity's past and present, and who will continue to shape its future.

Important Dates in the Life of Amelia Earhart

Born July 24 in Atchison, Kansas. — **1897**

1915 — Graduated from Hyde Park High School in Chicago, Illinois.

Served as nurse's aide at Spadina Military Hospital in Toronto, Ontario. — **1918**

1919 — Enrolled in Columbia University Extension to study medicine.

Took first plane ride. — **1920**

1921 — Took flying lessons and bought first plane.

Set women's altitude record of 14,000 feet. — **1922**

1923 — Engaged to Sam Chapman.

Moved with her mother to Medford, Massachusetts. — **1924**

As a passenger, became first woman to fly the Atlantic; wrote *20 Hrs. 40 Mins;* was first woman to make a solo round-trip transcontinental flight. — **1926** **1928**

1926 — Became social worker at Denison House in Boston.

Was elected first president of Ninety Nines; became vice president of Ludington Line, a commercial airline; set women's speed record of 181.19 miles an hour. — **1929** **1930**

1929 — Came in third in the first Women's Air Derby.

Wrote *The Fun of It;* became first woman to fly the Atlantic Ocean solo and first woman to fly the Atlantic Ocean twice; set women's record for fastest nonstop transcontinental flight—19 hours, 5 minutes. — **1932**

1931 — Married George Palmer Putnam.

1932 **1933** — Broke her own transcontinental record—17 hours, 7 minutes, 39 seconds.

Won third Harmon Trophy as America's Outstanding Airwoman. — **1934** **1935**

Disappeared at the age of thirty-nine during an attempt to fly around the world at the equator. — **1937**

1935 — Became first person to fly over Pacific Ocean from Hawaii to California; first person to fly from Los Angeles to Mexico City; first person to fly from Mexico City to Newark, New Jersey.

The Trailblazer

Heroes are extraordinary people. Trailblazers, they dare to go where no one has gone before. When Amelia Earhart became the first woman passenger to cross the Atlantic Ocean in an airplane, she also became America's national hero, a title she rated for the rest of her life. Her courage in daring to make the flight, her honesty in insisting that the pilot deserved all of the credit, her modesty in accepting the accolades, or praise, were traits that caught the fancy of the country and of the world, as well.

Not comfortable with undeserved praise, Earhart applied herself to earning respect for her own flying efforts. She began to set a series of solo flight records, some of which still stand.

Although Earhart always preferred to fly alone, she was among the first pilots to visualize the advantage of commercial air travel. She promoted the development of passenger airline service, still a fledgling in 1929. Representing Transcontinental Air Transport (TAT), later to become Trans World Airlines (TWA), Earhart lectured to business groups around the country. She also invested her own time and money in another new airline concept—shuttle service between New York City and Washington, D.C.

Fascinated though she was with flying, Earhart did have another consuming interest: She wanted women to be independent and self-reliant. Although she disliked being called a feminist, she nonetheless was a leader in the expanding feminist movement. She was part of a

Amelia Earhart was a trailblazer in many ways: as a woman, as a pilot, and as a speaker. Through her drive to be the best, she left a model for other women to follow.

growing group of women emerging in the late 1920s and early 1930s who wanted to take control of their lives and be something other than wife and helpmate to a man. Among the other women who led this feminist movement were Eleanor Roosevelt, the first U.S. president's wife to assert herself for women's rights; Babe Didrikson Zaharias, an Olympic athlete; Georgia O'Keeffe, painter; and Katharine Hepburn, actress.

Earhart worked most actively to achieve women's rights in aviation. Al-though she rarely joined organized groups, in 1929 Earhart became a charter member and the first president of the Ninety-Nines, a club of women pilots. The group was called the Ninety-Nines because it began with ninety-nine members. Earhart joined the group to show support for other women pilots. In a letter to Ruth Nichols inviting her to join the group, Earhart concluded with one of her favorite themes: "I do rather enjoy seeing women tackling all kinds of new problems—new for them, that is."[1] Earhart her-

Earhart with Eleanor Roosevelt, another influential woman who more directly appealed for women's rights.

self relished tackling new jobs, new kinds of airplanes, new routes, new interests.

As a pilot, a speaker, a writer, and a counselor of women at Purdue University, Earhart advocated equal rights for women. She advised women to pursue careers before and after marriage. She even suggested that marriage need not be their only goal—an unusual idea for those days.

Earhart's primary importance is twofold: She was a pioneer in aviation, and she was a role model. She led the way so that others could follow and go on to even greater achievements. She was her own best example of a woman who could, would, and did confront challenges with courage and confidence.

Amelia Earhart became a legend in her own time, and her legend lives on. Perhaps Charles Kuralt, television reporter and program host, crystallized the importance of Amelia Earhart when he said on the CBS television program *Sunday Morning*, "Trailblazers prepare the rest of us for the future."

Earhart will be remembered both as a role model and as a pioneer in aviation.

Chapter

1 Earhart's Widespread, but Shallow, Roots

Occasionally after giving a lecture or being honored at a banquet, Amelia Earhart was greeted by a stranger who would say, "I'm from your hometown." Earhart always replied, "Which one?" Moving marked her entire life. By the time she graduated from Chicago's Hyde Park High School in 1915, she had lived in five towns. She would live in eight more.

Born to Wealth

Amelia was born on July 24, 1897, in Atchison, Kansas, in the home of her mother's parents, a spacious brick and frame house on a bluff called Quality Hill. She was welcomed by a distinguished family. Her maternal grandfather, Judge Alfred Gideon Otis, was a retired judge of the U.S. District Court and president of the Atchison Savings Bank. Judge Otis traced his ancestry back to the American Revolutionary statesman James Otis.

Amy Otis, Amelia's mother, was the fourth of the Otises's eight children. Although Amy had been accepted by Vassar College in New York, a long siege with diphtheria thwarted her plans. When she finally recovered, she elected to travel by stagecoach with her father on his business

Amelia's parents, Amy and Edwin Earhart. Amy's father refused to allow the two to marry unless Edwin could prove his skills as a breadwinner.

trips into the Oklahoma and Utah territories rather than go to college. In 1890 on a trip to Colorado with her father, Amy climbed to the top of Pike's Peak, becoming the first woman to reach the summit.

Born to Poverty

Amelia's paternal grandparents were simple people. The Reverend David Earhart and his wife, Mary, had moved to Kansas in 1860. They had come from western Pennsylvania, where great-uncle John Earhart had been a soldier under George Washington.

Having settled in Sumner, three miles from Atchison, Reverend Earhart eked out a living for his wife and twelve children by serving his small congregation, teaching school, and farming. Amelia seldom saw this grandfather. She remembered only that he was a tall man with graceful hands. Her grandmother Mary had died before Amelia was born.

Edwin, Amelia's father, wanted to be a lawyer. After graduating from Thiel College in Pennsylvania at age eighteen, he worked his way through law school at the University of Kansas—stoking furnaces, tutoring classmates, shining shoes. He received his law degree in 1874.

Parents Meet and Marry

Edwin Earhart met Amy Otis at her presentation ball, a formal dance at which her parents introduced her to society. Edwin was not invited to the ball, but Amy's brother Mark, a classmate in law school, took him.

The good-looking, personable, and penniless lawyer and the attractive, winsome, and wealthy young debutante fell in love. Judge Otis, who expected his daughter to marry a neighbor from Quality Hill, refused to approve the match. Amy waited. Finally her father decreed that Edwin and Amy could marry when Edwin proved that he could earn fifty dollars a month for six successive months, not an easy achievement in 1890.

Amy's Independent Spirit

Amelia may have inherited her adventurous spirit from her mother, whose description of climbing Pike's Peak appears in Muriel Earhart Morrissey's Amelia, My Courageous Sister:

"I was the only female. I felt that several of the gentlemen deplored my presence as a restriction upon their language and possibly a deterrent to their speed. We made our last halt at about ten thousand feet. Here we left the burros in [the] charge of the second guide and proceeded on foot for the remainder of the ascent. We proceeded slowly because of the rarity of the atmosphere, and three of the gentlemen were afflicted with serious nose-bleeding and were forced to turn back. I reached the lookout platform below the Meteorological Station, just as the gray light was pierced by the sun's first rays. The men expressed wonder at my being there and both declared I was the first woman to have made the last hazardous quarter-mile climb."

Amelia with her younger sister, Muriel. From an early age, both girls preferred baseball and football to the more typical pursuits of girls—dolls and playing house.

As a claim settlement lawyer for the Rock Island Railroad, Edwin was paid a fee for each settlement rather than a straight salary. He finally met Judge Otis's demand in the fifth year. On October 16, 1895, Amy Otis married Edwin Earhart. Because his work was based in nearby Kansas City, the couple settled there in their wedding present, a two-story frame house selected, purchased, and furnished by Judge and Mrs. Otis.

The change from wealthy debutante to poor housewife tested Amy's endurance. Because she and Edwin could not afford the servants that she had taken for granted in her parents' home, Amy had to clean house, cook meals, and wash the dishes and the clothes. Most of all, she did not like being alone. To ease her frustrations, Edwin began to take her with him on his business trips, since he had free passes for the train. When the couple learned that they were to become parents, the Otises promptly insisted that Amy have her baby at their home in Atchison.

Childhood

Years later, when Amelia recalled her childhood, she wrote, "I am sure that I was a horrid little girl."[2] She must have been referring to her tomboyish ways. Both she and her sister, Muriel, two and a half years younger, scorned dolls. While they were visiting their grandparents during the Christmas holidays one year, Amelia wrote her father, "Muriel and I would like footballs this year, please. We need them especially, as we have plenty of baseballs, bats, etc."[3]

The sisters visited their grandparents frequently for long periods because Amy continued to travel with Edwin. During their early childhood Amelia and Muriel spent the school year in Atchison, where their grandparents enrolled them in a private school. Summer vacations they spent with their parents in Kansas City. They often traveled with Edwin and Amy, sometimes in a private railroad car assigned to Edwin.

In 1907, when Amelia was ten, her father was transferred to Rock Island's claims department in Des Moines, Iowa. For the first time he had the security of a regular salary. Edwin and Amy sold their house in Kansas City and moved to Des Moines. Amelia and Muriel remained in Atchison with the Otises until their parents were settled. Finally, in 1908 the sisters joined their parents in Des Moines permanently.

Reluctant to enroll her daughters in a public school, Amy hired a governess to teach them at home. The twenty-five-dollars-a-month salary was more than their budget could bear, however, so she soon enrolled them in the public school. Amy may have been disappointed, but Amelia and Muriel were delighted at the prospect of making new friends.

The Earharts' Family Life Is Disrupted

Over the years since Edwin and Amy had married, Edwin did little to change his in-laws' lack of faith in him. One year he used the money he and Amy had saved to pay their taxes to finance a trip to Washington. Then he sold the law books Judge Otis had given him to get money to pay their taxes. The judge was outraged. Another time Edwin earned an extra hundred dollars for settling a right-of-way dispute. Instead of depositing the money in savings as the Otises would have liked, he took Amy and their daughters to see the World's Fair in St. Louis, Missouri. The breach between the Otises and Edwin widened.

When Edwin was promoted to manager of the claims department, he spent most of his time working in the office. Although he was drawing a good salary, he disliked being confined to an office. And he was chafing at being criticized so much by the Otises. He began to drink, just a little with his coworkers at first. Then he drank more and more. His work began to suffer—minor mistakes that his secretary could cover, but he began to make major errors. Eventually he was fired.

After a month in a hospital for treatment of his alcoholism, Edwin returned home, confident that he could control his

Amelia at six. Amelia's early schooling took place in Atchison, where her grandparents enrolled her in private school.

weakness. Amy welcomed him with a set of carpentry tools; Amelia and Muriel, with a fishing pole for which they had earned money by picking strawberries. After only a few days, though, he began to drink again. He did not get his job back.

The Earharts' family problems were aggravated by Grandmother Otis's terminal illness late in 1911. Amy went to Atchison to care for her mother until Mrs. Otis died in February 1912. During those long weeks fourteen-year-old Amelia assumed the role of head of the family. With Amy gone and Edwin often drunk, Amelia made the household decisions.

By the time of Mrs. Otis's death, Edwin still had not found another job. Muriel recalled the tension within the family in her biography of Amelia:

(Above) Amelia, on stilts, and Muriel, on a swing. (Right, front row) Muriel, Amelia, and their parents (far right). At this age, Amelia was already taking on many of the household responsibilities from her mother.

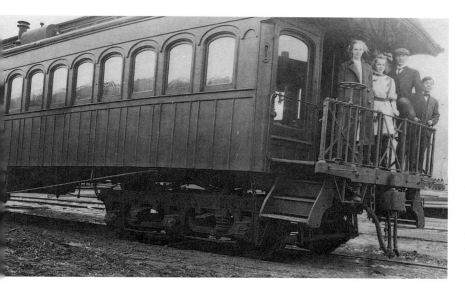

Amelia (left), Muriel, Edwin, and a porter on a railroad car in Atchison in 1911. Amelia's mother had moved to Atchison so that she could more easily nurse her terminally ill mother.

Just at this time Grandmother died, dividing the estate worth several hundred thousand dollars evenly among Mother and the other children. Dad regarded the will's instructions of Mother's share to be left in trust for twenty years or until his death as an insult.

Grandmother knew of Dad's drinking and was worried at the possibility of Dad's squandering Mother's share. All of Dad's old bitterness toward Mother's family became accentuated.[4]

Moving Again and Again and Again

In 1913 the Great Northern Railway finally hired Edwin as a freight office clerk. The job required that the family move to St. Paul, Minnesota. Amelia enrolled in Central High School as a junior; Muriel enrolled as a freshman. Three months later Edwin's boss asked him to investigate a train wreck in Albert Lea, a town in southern Minnesota. While the girls were help-ing him pack, Amelia discovered a bottle of whiskey hidden in his suitcase. She took it into the kitchen and poured it down the drain just as Edwin walked into the kitchen. Furious, he raised his arm to strike her. Hearing his angry voice, Amy rushed in and held his arm. Appalled at his near violence, Edwin apologized. He completed the investigation of the train wreck, but he did not get transferred to the claims department, as he had hoped.

After a long year in St. Paul, Edwin received an offer for a job in the claims office of the Burlington Railroad in Springfield, Missouri. The family moved again. When they arrived, dusty and tired, the man whom Edwin was to replace had decided not to retire after all. After spending the night in a cheap hotel, Amy made some decisions. Edwin must return to Kansas City, live with his sister, and set up a law practice. She and the girls would go to Chicago to stay with their friends the Shedds. When Edwin was solvent again, they would join him in Kansas City. He reluctantly agreed to the plan.

Standing for Equal Rights

At Ogontz, Amelia set out to change the discriminating membership system of the sororities, as remembered by Muriel Earhart Morrissey in Amelia, My Courageous Sister:

"Amelia was invited to join one of the three secret societies at the school. She enjoyed the carefully guarded ritual and the camaraderie of the members until she found that there were some girls at Ogontz who did not belong to any sorority. She urged the society to take in more girls, but the idea was not accepted. She then went to the headmistress, Abby A. Sutherland, and asked the faculty to approve four societies instead of three. Amelia felt that every girl ought to have the opportunity of belonging to a sorority.

I do not know the outcome of this crusade of Amelia's, but her concern for the out-group stemmed from the days at Hyde Park when she too had walked alone, and not from choice."

Edwin Earhart became an alcoholic after finding it increasingly difficult to live up to his in-laws' expectations. Although Edwin was a devoted family man, he simply could not keep a steady job.

The Shedds welcomed them with delight. Not wanting to impose, though, Amy found a small apartment that she could afford with the interest from her trust fund. Looking for a high school with a strong science department, Amelia investigated the schools within commuting distance. She decided on Hyde Park High School.

Although pleased with her chemistry class, Amelia was dismayed by her English class. The teacher was so nearly deaf that she could not conduct a class discussion. The students mocked her and answered her occasional question with nonsense that she could not hear. Disgusted with the students' cruelty and with a wasted class, Amelia wrote a petition requesting a capable teacher, but no one would sign it. Then she got special permission to spend the English period in the library, where she read four times as much literature as she would have read in class. The Hyde Park yearbook labeled Amelia "The girl in brown who walks alone." She graduated in 1915 but did not wait for graduation ceremonies or her diploma. Amy had decided that they should return to Kansas City.

Edwin met them with a plan to make them more prosperous. He wanted Amy to sue to break her mother's will. Persuading Amy took some time, for she did not like suing her own family, but she finally agreed. To their relief her mother's doctor testified that Mrs. Otis had been too ill when she had her lawyer prepare the will to understand that she was treating Amy as if she were incompetent. Unfortunately Amy's brother had mismanaged her trust, but she collected what remained—about sixty thousand dollars.

Becoming a Lady at Ogontz School

Amy could now afford to send Amelia to a university, but it was too late to enroll for the fall semester. On October 4, 1916, Amelia entered Ogontz School in Pennsylvania. Ogontz, a finishing school, trained young women in the social graces: how to sit, stand, and walk gracefully; how to stand in a receiving line; how to appreciate cultural events, such as those in nearby Philadelphia. The school also offered a college-preparatory curriculum. According to Muriel, "Amelia chose Ogontz because she wanted to transfer to Bryn Mawr," a nearby exclusive women's college.[5] Too, the years Amelia had spent in her grandparents' home had trained her to respect the conventions of polite behavior, and

Earhart at seventeen. A good student and a loner, Earhart enjoyed reading and chemistry.

Amy ran a formal household within the confines of her limited budget. Amelia "accepted as a matter of course the theory that to keep one's place in the social order one followed ongoing traditions," as biographer Jean Backus points out.[6] Amelia would later work alongside truck drivers, airplane mechanics, and illiterate immigrants, and she would do so graciously.

A Call to War Nurse Duty

In 1917 during Amelia's second Christmas vacation, she visited Muriel, who was in

Earhart in 1915 sports a graduation cap even though the family's move prevented her from attending graduation ceremonies.

instead she trained as a nurse's aide in Toronto. Then she reported to Spadina Military Hospital in Toronto. Amelia worked ten hours a day rubbing backs, scrubbing floors, changing beds, serving meals, and writing letters for soldiers. Appalled at the wounds—both physical and emotional—of the men, Amelia became a resolute, lifelong pacifist.

Some of the officers invited Amelia and Muriel to go to the airfields to watch training exercises. Amelia wanted to do more than just watch, but military rules forbade civilians' flying in military planes. She still went out to the field to watch whenever she had time.

Amelia's career as a nurse ended with the cessation of war on Armistice Day, November 11, 1918. She joined Muriel, who was studying at Smith College in Northampton, Massachusetts. For some time Amelia had been plagued by a chronic sinus infection that caused severe headaches. In 1919 doctors had no antibiotics; they could only operate to open and irrigate infected sinuses. A series of minor sinus operations forced Amelia to convalesce in Northampton in the spring of 1919.

Artistic and Scientific

To pass the time, Amelia took a five-week course in automotive mechanics with nine other women from Smith College. Still restless, she bought a five-string banjo from a pawnshop and took lessons from a local musician "for the fun of it." Muriel was not surprised at "the incongruity of the two activities because [Amelia] had always been artistic and impractical on one

school in Toronto, Ontario. When the pair went for walks down King Street, they passed Canadian and British soldiers who had been wounded in World War I. Amelia later wrote in her autobiography that she was stunned by the sight. "There for the first time I realized what the World War meant. Instead of new uniforms and brass bands, I saw men without arms and legs, men who were paralyzed and men who were blind."[7]

Amelia told her mother that she could not "bear the thought of going back to school and being so useless."[8] With Amy's consent, Amelia did not return to Ogontz;

A Budding Feminist

During her first year at Ogontz, Earhart began a scrapbook of clippings about successful career women. Muriel described the scrapbook in Amelia, My Courageous Sister:

"During the spring of Amelia's freshman year at Ogontz, the United States entered World War I. Because she felt that women traditionally were relegated to a secondary position in the conduct of war, she began her scrapbook on women's careers. She cut items from magazines and newspapers telling of women's achievements in fields usually considered a man's domain.

Amelia included an article dealing with an inquiry on legislation affecting women. The legislators were urged to remove restrictions that prohibited women holding property independently and to grant rights of inheritance. Amelia penciled: 'This method is not sound. Women will gain economic justice by proving themselves in all lines of endeavor, not by having laws passed for them.'"

Amelia in her nurse's aide outfit in 1917. Amelia's desire to help with the war effort proved a fateful opportunity—through the soldiers she nursed, she gained access to airplanes, and her lifelong fascination with flying began.

hand and scientific and intensely practical on the other."[9]

To help Amelia convalesce, Amy took the girls to Lake George in New York for the summer. By the end of their stay, Amelia was ready to get on with her life. Her work at the hospital in Toronto had interested her in becoming a doctor. In September 1919 she went to New York City to enroll in a premedical program at Columbia University Extension. She signed up for classes in chemistry, zoology, psychology—and French poetry "for fun." She wrote in her autobiography, "It took me only a few months to discover that I probably should not make the ideal physician. Though I liked learning all about medicine, particularly the experimental side, visions of its practical application floored me."[10]

Earhart in a bathing cap in 1919. Minor illness prevented her from returning to school at the end of the war, but she did a brief stint in medical school from 1919 to 1920.

Parents' Marriage in Trouble

When the semester ended in the spring of 1920, Earhart's parents were living in Los Angeles, but their marriage was foundering. Hoping that being a family of four again might strengthen the marriage, Edwin urged Amelia and Muriel to join them for the summer. Muriel decided that she could not afford a round-trip train ticket to California for just three months. Amelia agreed to join her parents, but she did not relish her role as peacemaker. She told Muriel (also known to the family as Pidge), "I'll see what I can do to keep Mother and Dad together until you finish college, Pidge, but after that, I'm going to come back here and live my own life."[11]

Just shy of her twenty-third birthday, Amelia again became head of the household, this time in the additional role of peacemaker. Hereafter, Edwin, Amy, and Muriel would all defer to Amelia's judgment and counsel.

2 Earhart Searches for Her Niche

When Amelia Earhart boarded the train for Los Angeles in June 1920, she planned first to try to mend the rift in her parents' marriage—just how, she was not sure. Then she thought that she might explore medical research at one of the universities in California. Before leaving for California, Earhart did not seem to have any definite goal or driving force in her life. She showed no

Earhart met Sam Chapman, a young engineer who boarded with her family, in Los Angeles. They found they shared many interests, and became engaged.

awareness of a need to help her parents financially, even though her mother's inheritance was almost exhausted, and her parents were again counting every dollar. Earhart had dated now and then, but she had not been seriously interested in any particular man. Although almost twenty-three years old, an age when most young women were settled on a job or marriage, she was still wandering rather aimlessly.

When she arrived in Los Angeles, Earhart was surprised to learn that Edwin had finally gained control of his alcoholism with the help of friends. Amy and Edwin were renting a large house on West Fourth Street. To supplement their income, they were renting rooms to three young men. One was Sam Chapman, an industrial engineer from Marblehead, Massachusetts. Earhart and Chapman soon discovered that they enjoyed several common interests—reading, seeing plays, swimming, playing tennis. Eventually Earhart and Chapman became engaged.

First Plane Ride

One activity they did not share was flying, which was fast becoming Earhart's favorite hobby. She took her first ride in a plane in

1920 at an air circus at a cost of ten dollars for ten minutes. Her pilot, Frank Hawks, later became famous for breaking speed records. Annoyed because Hawks insisted on taking another flier along to calm her in case she became frightened, Earhart nonetheless enjoyed the flight. She wrote later, "As soon as we left the ground, I knew I myself had to fly. Miles away I saw the ocean and the Hollywood hills seemed to peep over the edge of the cockpit, as if they were already friends."[12]

Earhart approached her father about flying lessons, but he could not afford the thousand dollars the entire course would cost. Undaunted, she got a job clerking in the office of the telephone company. On weekends she rode the streetcar to the end of the line and walked along the dusty road three miles to Kinner Airfield, an open field with a dirt runway and one hangar. Earhart clearly remembered those long walks:

> From then on the family scarcely saw me for I worked all the week and spent what I had of Saturday and Sunday at the airport a few miles from town. The trip there took more than an hour to the end of the carline, and then a walk of several miles along the dusty highway. In those days it was really necessary for a woman to wear breeks [breeches, or pants] and a leather coat. The fields were dusty and the plane hard to climb into. Flyers dressed the part in semi-military outfits and in order to be as inconspicuous as possible, I fell into the same style.[13]

Earhart made another change in her appearance, although for a more practical reason. Her waist-long light brown hair would not tuck under a flight helmet, yet

Earhart in her working clothes in 1920. She worked at a telephone company to earn money for flying lessons and cut off her waist-long hair to make it easier to wear a pilot's helmet.

she could not have it flying behind in an open cockpit. In *The Fun of It* she told how she solved her problem: "I had been snipping inches off my hair secretly, but I had not bobbed it lest people think me eccentric. For in 1920 it was very odd indeed for a woman to fly, and I had tried to remain as normal as possible in looks."[14]

Earhart Learns to Fly

Convinced that she would be more comfortable learning from a woman, Earhart found Neta Snook, the first woman graduate of the Curtiss School of Aviation. Earhart had her first lesson from Snook on January 2, 1921. She took lessons thereafter as often as she could afford them, although Snook would give her lessons on credit. The first few lessons took place on the ground: learning the structure of the plane, the purposes of the equipment inside the cockpit, the basic principles of flight. Then Snook, in her own two-seater Canuck plane, took Earhart aloft. Earhart sat in the front cockpit, Snook in the back. Earhart explained the teaching routine in *20 Hrs. 40 Mins.*:

> New students were instructed in planes with dual controls; the rudder and stick in the front cockpit are connected with those in the rear so that any false move the student makes can be corrected by the instructor. Every move is duplicated and can be felt by both flyers. One lands, takes off, turns, all with an experienced companion in command.[15]

Buying a Plane

Although Earhart was far from flying solo, she soon wanted her own plane. Bert Kinner's prototype of the plane he would later produce and sell, the Airster, was available, but Snook and some of the male pilots warned Earhart that the little plane was unstable and underpowered and that one cylinder of the three-cylinder engine often clogged, stalling the engine. Earhart disregarded their advice, bought the plane for two thousand dollars with Amy's help, had it painted yellow, and called it the *Canary.* Now that she owned her own plane, Earhart wanted to look as the other pilots looked. To her breeches and knee-high boots she added a leather helmet,

goggles, and a leather knee-length jacket, which she slept in a couple of nights to make it look rumpled and worn.

Snook continued giving Earhart lessons, but now in the *Canary.* On one flight the engine stalled. They landed in Cora and Bert Kinner's cabbage patch.

Earhart in full flight gear. Even before she could fly solo, Earhart knew she wanted to be a pilot and bought her first plane.

Earhart's flight teacher, Neta Snook (above, left), and Earhart stand in front of Earhart's first plane, the Kinner Airster she dubbed Canary *(below). Neta often nagged Amelia for not being a careful pilot.*

Neither was hurt. A few flights later they flew the *Canary* six miles from Kinner's field to Goodyear Field to see a new plane built by Donald Douglas. As they took off to return, the *Canary* did not climb fast enough to clear a line of eucalyptus trees. If Earhart nosed down to gain speed, they would slam into the trees; if she nosed the plane up, it would stall. She chose to pull up, the engine stalled, and they crashed. A broken propeller and damaged landing gear were the only casualties.

Snook and Earhart were sometimes at odds over Earhart's carelessness. Snook was a careful pilot who anticipated problems. Just after Earhart had taken off one morning, Snook shouted to ask if Earhart had checked to see if the gas tank was full.

Earhart shouted back that she had not because Kinner always filled the tank every evening. Without another word Snook took over the controls and landed the plane. A worried Bert Kinner came running to meet them. The gas truck had not come the previous afternoon, so he had not filled the plane's gas tank.

First Solo and First Record

Before Earhart was ready to solo, Neta Snook retired to get married. Earhart hired a former army flight instructor, John "Monte" Montijo. She insisted that he teach her stunt flying before she soloed. She had no plans to do stunt work, but she thought it would better prepare her for emergencies. One day they practiced takeoffs and landings for a while. Then he climbed out and waved her on.

As she was gliding up the runway preparing to take off, the right wing suddenly dropped. Reacting quickly, she stopped the plane. A shock absorber had snapped. After getting a quick repair, she took off, this time lifting the plane into the air. She flew to five thousand feet, did some maneuver exercises, and came down to make a terrible, bouncy landing. The quality of the landing did not matter to Earhart. She had finally soloed.

For the next year Earhart flew whenever she had time and the money for gas. She worked at various jobs to support her flying—truck driver, commercial photographer, companion to an invalid. In October 1922 at an air meet Earhart set a new women's altitude record when she flew the *Canary* to fourteen thousand feet—her first record.

In 1923 she qualified for the only pilot's license available then, awarded by the Federation Aeronautique Internationale,

---

Stunt Flying

In The Fun of It, *Earhart explained why she asked her flying instructor, Monte Montijo, to teach her stunt flying:*

"The fundamental stunts taught to students are slips, stalls, and spins—three S's instead of R's. Loops, barrel rolls and variations and combinations of many kinds are included depending on the instruction desired. The Army, Navy and Marines practice intricate and specialized maneuvers, performing many of them in formation.

A knowledge of some stunts is judged necessary to good flying. Unless a pilot has actually recovered from a stall, has actually put his plane into a spin and brought it out, he cannot know accurately what those acts entail. He should be familiar enough with abnormal positions of his craft to recover without having to think how."

of which the National Aeronautic Association (NAA) was a member. As Earhart pointed out, "It wasn't really necessary to have any license at this period. People just flew, when and if they could, in anything which would get off the ground."[16] The license would be, however, an impressive credential to enhance her status as a pilot.

Moving to Boston

While Earhart's budding career as a flier was progressing well, her parents' reconciliation was not. In 1924 they decided that they could no longer live together. Edwin filed for an uncontested divorce.

Because Amy had not liked living in California, Amelia decided to take her to

From the start, Amelia was a trailblazer. Shortly after her first solo flight she set a new women's altitude record, flying the Canary *to fourteen thousand feet.*

Medford, Massachusetts, a suburb of Boston, where Muriel was then teaching junior high school English. At first Amelia planned to fly her mother in the *Canary*, but Amelia's chronic sinus infection had been aggravated by her open-cockpit flying. She was plagued by severe headaches every time she flew. Reluctantly, she sold the *Canary* and bought a yellow Kissel Kar, a long, sporty convertible, which she called the Yellow Peril.

The Earharts traveled leisurely. Unpaved roads dictated a slow pace, and gas stations and hotels were infrequent. Yet those conditions did not bother Earhart or her mother, for they were sightseeing: Sequoia National Park, Yosemite National Park, Lake Louise in Banff National Park in Canada, Yellowstone National Park. They sidetracked to visit friends and relatives along the way. Their meandering seven-thousand-mile trip from California to Massachusetts took six weeks.

Earhart's exchanging her plane for a car had pleased Sam Chapman. He was ready for her to settle down and marry him. To Chapman a wife was a helpmate who would keep his house, rear his children, cook his meals, and wash his clothes. To do these chores, she would stay at home, not fly all over the country. Although Earhart was not willing to accept that role, Chapman regarded the sale of her plane as a hopeful sign. He quit his job in Los Angeles and followed her to Massachusetts.

After arriving in Medford, Earhart suffered another sinus infection and entered the hospital. Driving with the top down on her car had aggravated the condition again. This time a surgeon removed a piece of bone from her nose so that her sinuses could drain. When pressure in her

Working with Immigrants

For years Earhart had heard that America was a melting pot. In The Fun of It *she described the melting that she saw firsthand:*

"The people whom I met through Denison House were as interesting as any I have ever known. The neighborhood was mostly Syrian and Chinese with a few Italians and Irish mixed in. I had never been privileged to know much about how people other than Americans lived. Now I discovered manner and modes very different from those with which I was familiar. Under my very nose Oriental ideas and the home-grown variety were trying to get along together. The first time I saw, sitting on a modern gas stove, one of the native clay cooking dishes used for centuries by the Syrians, I felt I was seeing evidence of the blending process.

Changes which words underwent in meaning and pronunciation were very interesting to me. The fruit which boarding houses have justly or injustly made famous was usually pronounced pru-ins in two syllables, instead of prunes. The word 'fresh' covered all degrees of misconduct and could be a slight rebuke or an insult. It was funny to hear of a 'fresh baby' instead of a naughty one. The Chinese called it 'flesh' but kept the same meaning. I wonder what Americans do to foreign words."

head was relieved, she was pain free for the first time in years, although the infection would flare up occasionally throughout the rest of her life.

Job Hunting

Thinking again that she might go into medical research, Earhart returned to Columbia University in New York in 1924 for the fall and spring terms to take science classes. Low on money, she went back to Medford in 1925. That summer she taught English to foreign students at a University of Massachusetts extension program. The job required her to teach at different locations in the Boston area. With a salary that barely covered her transportation and left no money for plane rentals, she looked for another job.

Earhart answered an ad in a Boston newspaper for a part-time instructor to teach English to immigrants at Denison House, a social service agency in Boston. Marion Perkins, director of the agency, interviewed Earhart and hired her immediately, in spite of her lack of social work training. Perkins liked Earhart's credentials. She already had experience teaching English to foreigners, and she had excellent references from a previous employer and from Sam Chapman. On Earhart's application form, Perkins wrote, "an extremely interesting girl—very unusual vocab—is a philosopher—wants to write—does write—holds a sky pilot's license!"[17]

Earhart plunged eagerly into her new work in October 1926. She was making more money, she had fewer expenses, and she had free weekends to fly. She taught the immigrants English, helped them solve their personal problems, visited them in their homes, and took the children for rides in the Yellow Peril. Perkins soon promoted her to full-time resident staff at a monthly salary of sixty dollars.

Although Earhart had finally found a vocation that interested and challenged her, she hated filling out forms and writing reports. Perkins often had to edit Earhart's reports to add the details that Earhart had been too impatient to include before submitting them to the agency's board of directors.

Refuses Marriage for Flying and Career

Earhart's move to Denison House marked a change in her relationship with Sam

Earhart with children from Denison House in Boston. Even though Earhart was a loner by nature, she was excellent with the immigrant families at Denison, helping them learn English and solve personal problems.

Flying Was a Passion

In Letters from Amelia *Jean L. Backus describes Earhart's reaction to her first ride in a plane:*

"From a field off Wilshire Boulevard the plane lifted over the friendly Hollywood hills, and at two or three hundred feet up Amelia knew she had to fly.

Nothing had prepared her for the physical and emotional impact of flight. No other urge, no intellectual, sexual, or social excitement ever involved or moved her as totally as soaring into the subtle environment where her most secret self was free of earthly concerns and subject to no human influence but her own. Here was the ultimate happiness, the physical and sensual as well as intellectual thrill for which no partner was needed, and no words were adequate."

Chapman. He was dismayed because he thought she was becoming too involved with the children. The more he pressed her to marry him, the further she retreated. Thinking that she might resent the irregular hours he worked, he offered to change jobs or even professions. According to Muriel, Amelia only spurned this gesture. "Instead of being impressed by his eagerness to please her, Amelia was annoyed. She did not want to tell Sam what he should do. Amelia knew what she wanted and expected to achieve, married or single."[18] Eventually Earhart told Chapman that she would not marry him, but they remained good friends.

What Earhart wanted to do was to fly. On weekends she had time to fly, but she had no plane. Fortunately Bert Kinner had set up a sales agency in Boston, and he let her fly his new model Kinner Airster in return for demonstrating it. When she had

time but no money for gas, she still went to the airfield to talk with other pilots and to watch the mechanics work on the planes. Occasionally she put on overalls and worked with them. Getting more and more serious about flying, she joined the National Aeronautic Association in Boston.

When Earhart chose flying rather than marriage, she was no doubt thinking of the kind of flying she had been doing—taking an occasional trip, perhaps aiming for another record, but mostly flying for the freedom and enchantment that always thrilled her in the air. Her job left her weekends for flying. Being a resident counselor at Denison House gave her the independence she could not have had if she were still living with her mother and her sister. And her job was shaping into a career in social work. In 1927 Earhart was finally organizing her life into a pattern that she favored.

3 The *Friendship* Flight

On May 20–21, 1927, a pilot Earhart had never met set the stage for disrupting her orderly life. The aviation world—indeed, almost the entire world—celebrated his achievement: Charles Augustus Lindbergh had flown solo across the Atlantic Ocean, the first pilot ever to do so. His feat challenged other fliers. Within months fourteen people, including three women, had died trying to duplicate his flight.

The Search for a Representative American Woman

A plan for a woman to cross the Atlantic evolved in the spring of 1928. A wealthy American socialite living in England, Mrs. Amy Guest, wanted to be the first woman to make this flight, even if only as a passenger. She quietly bought the trimotor Fokker that Commander Richard E. Byrd had flown on his expedition to the North Pole. Guest named the plane *Friendship* because she hoped that her flight would further link the United States and England as friendly nations. When her family learned of her plan, they persuaded her not to undertake so dangerous a journey. Reluctantly, she decided to sponsor an American

woman to replace her as passenger. But who? Guest asked her lawyer, David Layman, for help in finding someone who could represent American women.

George Palmer Putnam, a grandson who worked at the G. P. Putnam's Sons Publishing Company, heard about the

Charles Lindbergh stands before the Spirit of St. Louis, *the plane he flew solo across the Atlantic Ocean. Lindbergh's flight would inspire a plan for a woman to repeat the journey.*

proposed venture from Commander Byrd's former pilot, Bernt Balchen. Putnam had published the successful *We*, Lindbergh's account of his solo flight across the Atlantic, and he wanted to publish another best-seller. After talking with Layman, Putnam asked his friend Hilton Railey, head of a public relations firm in Boston, to search for a representative American woman. Both of them sensed the chance for another big publicity coup. Railey asked Rear Admiral Reginald K. Belknap, who belonged to the Boston branch of the National Aeronautic Association, if he knew a woman who flew. Belknap did not actually know Earhart, but she had impressed him at association meetings: She seemed to take flying seriously, and she was still flying at Dennison Airport in Boston.

Railey called Earhart at Denison House that afternoon. In her account of the telephone call from Railey, she wrote:

> I was working as usual around Denison House. The neighborhood was just piling in for games and classes and I was as busy as could be. I remember when called to the phone I replied I couldn't answer unless the message was more important than entertaining many little Chinese and Syrian children. The word came assuring me it was.[19]

Railey was pleasant and businesslike, but vague. Would Earhart be interested in a proposed aviation project that might involve danger? Curious, she agreed to meet him that evening.

When Railey saw Earhart, he immediately thought that she looked enough like Charles Lindbergh to be his sister—an unexpected publicity plus. After cautioning her to consider this meeting confidential, he explained Guest's plan. Earhart impressed him with her composure, serious sense of purpose, and attractive appearance. He was confident that Earhart would fit Guest's idea of the representative American woman.

Ten days later Earhart took the train to New York City to be interviewed by Guest's representatives: Putnam, who had appointed himself chairman of the selection committee, Layman, and John S. Phipps, Guest's brother. They told her that the pilot would receive twenty thousand dollars; the mechanic, five thousand; and she, the passenger, nothing. Her pay would be the glory of the adventure. Earhart agreed to the terms.

Preparations for the Flight

Earhart returned to Denison House. Two days later she received a note from Guest and a contract drawn by Layman. Perhaps as compensation for not being paid, Earhart was to captain the crew, and her decisions were to be accepted without question. William Stultz would pilot the plane; Louis Gower would be his alternate, and Louis "Slim" Gordon, the mechanic.

Preparations for the flight progressed amid much secrecy. Another American woman, Mabel Boll, and a German woman, Thea Rasche, were also planning Atlantic flights. Boll, who knew Bill Stultz, had tried to get him to pilot her plane. When he told Commander Byrd of her offer, Byrd advised him to stay with Earhart. Too many flights would reduce the news value of Earhart's attempt. The *Friendship* had to beat its competitors.

While Earhart continued to work at Denison House, mechanics at a Boston

Earhart wrote what she called "popping off letters" to her parents before departing on her transatlantic flight. They were to receive them only if she did not survive the journey.

hangar adapted the *Friendship* for ocean flight. Pontoons replaced landing wheels. Extra gas tanks replaced passenger seats, raising the total fuel capacity to about nine hundred gallons—enough to give them a flight range over the Atlantic from Newfoundland to England, approximately thirty-five hundred miles. Golden wings and an orange fuselage would make the plane easier to see if it went down at sea.

Earhart had not said a word about the flight even to her parents or her sister. She did confide in two people. She asked Sam Chapman to tell Amy and Muriel as soon as the plane started across the ocean. Earhart also told Perkins, who would need to replace Earhart on the staff for the summer program at Denison House.

Earhart wrote her will, put it into her safe-deposit box, and told Chapman of its location. After all debts had been paid, whatever was left would go to her mother. To Amy and to Edwin she wrote what she called "popping off letters," which they were to receive only if she did not survive the trip.

To her father she wrote:

Hooray for the last grand adventure! I wish I had won, but it was worth while anyway. You know that.

I have no faith that we'll meet anywhere again, but I wish we might. Anyway, good-by and good luck to you.

Affectionately, yr dotor,
Meel

To her mother she wrote, "My life has really been very happy, and I didn't mind contemplating its end in the midst of it."[20]

These letters she gave to Putnam for safekeeping. Since she survived the flight, her parents never saw them.

The *Friendship* Takes Off

In 1928 meteorologists depended on ships at various points on the seas to send them weather reports by radio. For an entire week reports of bad weather kept the *Friendship* crew in Boston. Finally, late on June 1 meteorologist Doc Kimball notified the crew that the weather was favorable at both Boston and Trepassey, Newfound-land, their departure point for England. After rising at 3:30 A.M. on June 4 Earhart met the crew at an all-night diner to fill thermoses with coffee for the men and co-coa for her and to buy sandwiches.

Waiting at T Wharf in Boston Harbor were Railey and Putnam, who gave the crew a sack of oranges. The tugboat *Sadie Rose* ferried them all out to the *Friendship*, which was tied to the mooring float beyond the pier. Earhart, Stultz, and Gower climbed into the plane, while Gordon balanced on the pontoons to spin the propellers. Within minutes Stultz had all three engines running. The plane sped across the water, but Stultz could not nose it up into the air.

Keeping the Flight Secret

To forestall anyone else's taking off before the Friendship *could, the crew was pledged to secrecy, as Putnam explained in his biography of Earhart,* Soaring Wings:

"The intention from the first was to keep the plans secret, because the deluge of curiosity that would follow any leakage would hamper progress. And so, because AE was pretty well known around the Boston flying fields, she kept away while the ship was being conditioned. She had no chance to take part in any of the test flying and actually the first time she was off the water in the ship was the Sunday morning of the start.

Her first sight of the *Friendship* was of it jacked up among the shadows of an East Boston hangar, with mechanics and welders working on the struts for the pontoons that were to replace its wheels. She liked the look of the ship's golden wings with their spread of seventy-two feet. She saw that the red-orange of the fuselage, which blended with the gold of the wings, was a wise choice of color for, if the flight had to come down at sea, a boat, if any, could sight orange at a greater distance than any other color."

Discarding a five-gallon tank of gas was not enough; the plane was still too heavy. Gower knew the next step. Stultz turned back to pass the mooring float, where Gower jumped off. The absence of his 168 pounds lightened the plane enough for takeoff. They were on their way.

The *Friendship* was scarcely airborne when Earhart made the Boston and then worldwide headlines. Putnam had ended the secrecy. Amy and Muriel read about the event in the paper before Chapman could get to Medford to tell them. They were besieged by reporters. Amy, who believed that well-bred people were written about in newspapers only in their birth notices and obituaries, wanted to dismiss the reporters, but Muriel persuaded her to cooperate with them.

The crew had no problems until they neared Halifax, Nova Scotia, where fog forced them to land for the night. Earhart wired her mother, "Know you will understand why I could not tell plans of flight. Don't worry. No matter what happens it will have been worth the trying. Love, A."

Amy wired back, "We are not worrying. Wish I were with you. Good luck and cheerio. Love, Mother"[21]

They took off the next morning and landed in Trepassey, where bad weather kept them for thirteen long days. On the evening of June 16 Earhart and Gordon were playing a hand of rummy. They could hear Stultz, who had been drinking steadily, pacing and swearing in the room above them. Gordon kept assuring Earhart that Stultz would be all right once

Earhart at the door of the plane Friendship. *The plan for Earhart to be the first woman to cross the Atlantic was pursued with great secrecy, and generated a lot of publicity for Earhart.*

Earhart takes off from Boston Harbor in Friendship *in 1928. Although a huge publicity success, the flight disappointed Earhart, who felt she got credit for doing nothing.*

he was seated at the controls of the plane. Not convinced, Earhart was debating whether to send for Gower to replace Stultz when the telegraph operator brought her a message: The weather would be favorable the next day.

Destination: Ireland!

Early the next morning she and Gordon poured cold water over Stultz and forced him to drink hot black coffee. They led him to the plane and sat him down before the controls. Appearing alert and confident, Stultz taxied across the bay and into the wind. The plane would not lift into the air. He turned his head and looked back at Earhart. She nodded, and he tried again. This time he got the speed up to fifty-five, and they were airborne. They had changed their destination to Ireland, because Trepassy could spare only enough fuel to bring their total up to seven hundred gallons.

About three hundred miles out they flew into a squall—fog, snow, driving rain. Finally they passed beyond the storm into clear weather. Earhart wrote in her log, "View too vast, too lovely for words. Light of our exhaust is beginning to show pink as the last glow in the sky. I am kneeling here by the chart table gulping in beauty."[22]

Ships Helped Planes Navigate

As the Friendship *neared the end of the Atlantic flight, Earhart tried to "bomb" a passing ship with a message tied to two oranges asking for its location, as she told in* The Fun of It:

"'Mess' expressed our situation as well as any single word I could think of at the time—our puzzlement [about where they were], our helplessness with a diminishing fuel supply, our exasperation at our inability to communicate with the ship just below us.

It turned out the ship was the *America*, commanded by Captain Field. Later he told me that every time he had learned of a contemplated crossing by air he had seen to it that bearings were painted on the deck every two hours in the hope that the flyers might come his way. But none ever had. Of our flight he had heard nothing in advance so his paint pots were not in readiness. For this lack of preparedness he afterwards apologized to me profusely, and, I understand, has since kept cans of paint ever ready to serve in a similar emergency."

She pulled on a fur-lined flight suit to protect herself from the cold. As they used fuel, the plane got lighter, and they could go up to ten thousand feet to escape some of the bad weather below them. After several hours of flying, one of the engines began to cough. Then their radio failed. They thought that they must be nearing land. Finally they passed a ship beneath them, but they could not determine its direction. Earhart began to wonder: "Instead of its course paralleling ours, as we thought it ought to, it was going directly across our path. Its action was unpleasantly puzzling. After all, were we lost?"[23] Stultz circled over it while Earhart wrote a note asking the captain to paint the ship's position on the deck. She tied the note to two oranges and dropped the bundle, but

it missed the ship. They flew on because they could not spare any more fuel.

They were down to an hour's supply of gas. After about half an hour they saw a fleet of fishing boats sailing ahead of them in the same direction. They followed the boats, and finally they saw land.

Landing in Wales

Stultz brought the plane down and landed in the water—twenty hours and forty minutes after they had left Trepassey. They thought that they were off the shore of Ireland.

Some men working along the shore looked up, saw the plane, and bent to

(Above) Crowds wait to greet Earhart upon her arrival at Burry Port, in southern Wales. (Below) Earhart shortly after her arrival.

their work again. The crew's shouts for help did not reach them. Earhart leaned out a window and waved a towel at them. One man took off his shirt and waved back to her. Finally a man rowed out to the plane. They were at Burry Port, in southern Wales. Stultz rode back with the man to wire Railey, who had boarded a ship for Southampton, England, the day the crew left Boston. After sending a message to Putnam, Stultz arranged for refueling so that they could fly on to Southampton. Eventually a launch came to get Earhart and Gordon.

Railey and some reporters soon arrived from Southampton. Earhart, the center of attention, was mobbed by all two thousand residents of Burry Port and the

Reactions from the Press

The comments about the Friendship *flight in both American and foreign newspapers were mixed—some good, some bad. In* Amelia Earhart, *biographer Doris Rich lists samples of each kind:*

"As an aviator [Earhart] was commended for her 'unquenchable determination to go on attempting the hitherto unachieved, no matter how great the dangers' and for her intent 'to render service to commercial aviation, not to make a sensation.' She had not failed 'to bring home to everyone the fine spirit of audacity shown by her sex in this age.'

Criticism was minimal, the most cutting in the *Church Times:* 'The voyage itself is a remarkable achievement made possible by the skill and courage of the pilot. As the *Evening Standard* has properly pointed out, "[Earhart's] presence added no more to the achievement than if the passenger had been a sheep."' "

reporters. Finally someone thought to give the crew food and let them sleep for a few hours. First Earhart sent two cables, one to her mother and one to Marion Perkins. Both said only, "Love, Amelia." The next morning the crew received several telegrams, including one to Earhart from President Calvin Coolidge: "To you the first woman successfully to span the North Atlantic by air the great admiration of myself and the United States."[24]

England Welcomes the Heroes

After the *Friendship* had been refueled, Earhart, Stultz, Gordon, and Railey climbed aboard. Also accompanying them was a reporter from the *New York Times*, with whom Putnam had arranged a con-

tract for Earhart to write articles. After circling above Burry Port once in salute, they flew to Southampton, with Earhart at the controls part of the way. Besides hundreds of people wanting to see Lady Lindy, as they were already calling her, were Guest and her son. In meeting Guest, Earhart crystallized in her mind one of the primary purposes of the *Friendship* flight: "More than ever then did I realize how essentially this was a feminine expedition, originated and financed by a woman, whose wish was to emphasize what her sex stood ready to do."[25]

When the crew, still wearing their flight clothes, reached the Hyde Park Hotel in London, people pushed and shoved as they tried to see Earhart. Photographers and reporters swarmed into her room. She tried repeatedly to give all credit to Stultz, saying, "I was just baggage, a bag of potatoes."[26] She finally sent a reply to President Coolidge: "The crew of the *Friendship* desire to express their deep appreciation of your Excellency's gracious message. Success entirely due to skill of Mr. Stultz."[27]

Lady Mary Heath, one of England's most prominent pilots, invited Earhart for an early morning flight in her plane, an Avro Avian, a small, single-engine aircraft. When she mentioned that it was for sale, Earhart asked to buy it on credit. The book she was to write for Putnam would surely pay for the plane. The Avro was lowered and tied to the deck of the ship on which Earhart sailed home.

A few newspapers, both American and British, considered Earhart a foolhardy publicity seeker. Most of the press, however, had only praise for her. Guest thought that the flight had achieved her purpose and that Earhart had been a gracious American ambassador to England.

Sailing Home

After ten days of hectic celebrations, the crew boarded the *Roosevelt* to sail home. In *20 Hrs. 40 Mins.* Earhart described the voyage: "On June 28 we began our first ocean voyage, embarking on the SS *President Roosevelt* of the United States Lines. It was really our first ocean voyage and it was then that we came to realize how much water we had passed over in the *Friendship*."[28]

Like a showman, Putnam had staged the elaborate reception awaiting them in New York. They were met by Putnam and his wife, Dorothy; Grover Whalen, the mayor's official greeter for New York City; Commander Byrd and his aide in dress uniform; and a crowd of five thousand cheering fans. Sitting in the back seat of an open convertible, Earhart, Stultz, and Gordon were treated to a ticker tape

Pictured, from left, are Amy Guest, the wealthy socialite who originally wanted to make the transatlantic flight; Lou Gordon, the mechanic; Earhart; William Stultz, the pilot; and Mrs. Foster Welsh, mayor of Southampton.

After their historic flight, the crew was invited to celebrate in cities across the United States. (Left) Stultz, Earhart, and Gordon during a parade in New York. (Below) Earhart accepts congratulations from her mother in Boston.

parade up Broadway to city hall to meet more dignitaries, including a representative of President Coolidge. The extravaganza continued for two more days.

Thirty-two cities invited the crew to come for celebrations. They chose three—Boston, Medford, and Chicago—for more parades and receptions. The constant attention and celebration were more than Stultz could take. In Chicago he disappeared, and Earhart never saw him again. Putnam, wearing a flying helmet and goggles, sat beside Earhart in the open car. Everybody assumed that he was Stultz.

Exhausted, Earhart returned to New York, where she hoped to get some rest. Then she would write the promised book about the flight. After completing that obligation, she would return to her work at Denison House.

4 Changing Directions

Earhart had really believed that once the celebrations were over, she would return to the life she had known before the Atlantic flight. Invitations and fan letters kept pouring in, however. And she had to write the articles for the *New York Times*. According to her contract with Guest, the money paid her by the *Times* would go to defray the costs of the flight. Wanting to take early advantage of the publicity, Putnam, who had appointed himself Earhart's manager, was pressuring her to write her book about the flight immediately. He had promised her that she would make thousands of dollars from the sale of the book. He had begun scheduling lectures for her even before she left England, and he was planning some product endorsements for her. Earhart was a world-famous celebrity now, and Putnam knew it, even if she did not.

Writing Her Book

Putnam gave Earhart a little help when he invited her to stay with him and his wife, Dorothy, at their home in Rye, New York, while she wrote the book. Not only could she work in privacy, but he would provide a secretary as well.

Earhart during her stay with the Putnams in Rye, New York, where Putnam hoped to keep an eye on Earhart and encourage her to write her book. She is pictured with Putnam's son David at the beach near the Putnam home.

The Putnams' spacious home was in a secluded area where the reporters could not get to Earhart. When she learned that reporters were still bothering Amy and Muriel, she wrote her mother, "Just opened your letter. Can't understand. I am protected here. No one gets to me. If a Hearst reporter annoys you, wire me and I can have it stopped. Don't worry, but be careful about telling people whereabout I am."[29]

Earhart settled down to work on her account of the *Friendship* flight, which she titled *20 Hrs. 40 Mins.*, the time it had taken the crew to fly from Trepassey to Burry Port. She took about six weeks of writing steadily to complete the book. She dedicated the book to her hostess, Dorothy Putnam. Although Earhart's writing was competent, much of *20 Hrs. 40 Mins.* reads like a daily log. Only occasionally does it reflect her excitement in the adventure. She did express one aspect of flying that would always intrigue her—the beauty she saw when she looked out of the plane's window. She described a sunset over the ocean: "Marvelous shapes in white stand out, some trailing shimmering veils. The clouds look like icebergs in the distance. The highest peaks of the fog mountains are tinted pink with the setting sun. The hollows are grey and shadowy."[30]

In her book Earhart introduced another theme that would appear repeatedly in her writing and speaking: equal rights for women. Although she had lacked the navigational skills necessary for the *Friendship* flight, she maintained, "There should be no line between men and women as far as piloting is concerned." A few pages later she added, "Inheritance, training and environment seem to make women less aggressive than men, although in real courage I think they are equals."[31]

In her book 20 Hrs. 40 Mins, *Earhart expressed her belief that men and women are equally courageous.*

Earhart tried to read every one of the two hundred or so letters that she was still receiving every day—letters of praise, marriage proposals, pleas for money, requests for autographs, occasionally a crank letter, and many letters from admiring children. Occasionally Putnam brought people to talk with her: "Between chapters I talked to editors, promoters, airline operators, and educators with propositions generous, preposterous, or inviting. Before any commitments were made, the book was completed. Clearly, it was time to get into the air again."[32]

First Transcontinental Flight

Eager to fly the Avro Avian, the small plane she had brought back from England, Earhart decided to fly it from New York to California. She wanted to see the National Air Races in Los Angeles and to talk with her father and some flying acquaintances. She was not thinking beyond California, but she knew that she had to make some decisions. Earhart described her uncertainty about the future in *The Fun of It:* "I still had no plan for myself. Should I return to social work, or find something to do in aviation? I didn't know —or care. For the moment all I wished to do in the world was to be a vagabond—in the air." [33]

Since Earhart did not want reporters following her, she told only two people, her mother and a friend from New York, about her planned trip. Even with them she was vague about the date she would leave. Then early on August 29, 1928, she packed her suitcase, gathered some maps, and took off for California.

Air navigation maps in 1928 were somewhat sketchy and not always accurate. Earhart took some with her, plus some

---

Writing About the *Friendship* Flight

As Earhart wrote 20 Hrs. 40 Mins., *she considered some of the questions fans had asked her about the flight:*

"As I look back on the flight I think two questions have been asked me most frequently. First: Was I afraid? Secondly: What did I wear?

I'm sorry to be a disappointment in answering the first query. But I honestly wasn't [afraid]. Of course I realized there was a measure of danger. Obviously I faced the possibility of not returning when first I considered going. Once faced and settled there really wasn't any good reason to refer to it again.

I chose to take with me only what I had on. Just my old flying clothes, comfortably, if not elegantly, battered and worn. High laced boots, brown broadcloth breeks [breeches, or pants], white silk blouse with a red necktie (rather antiquated!) and a companionable ancient leather coat. A homely brown sweater accompanied it. A light leather flying helmet and goggles completed the picture.

When it was cold I wore a heavy fur-lined flying suit which covers one completely from head to toe, shoes and all."

road maps, which were sometimes more helpful. She was already familiar with the way bewildered pilots tried to stay on course over unknown territory. They often used landmarks such as roads, towers, rivers, and railroad tracks. She described her usual direction-finding technique in *The Fun of It:*

> My compass reads due west. I have been flying for more than an hour. Speed 100 m.p.h. In half an hour, if the course is correct and I have allowed properly for winds, I ought to cross a river which is fifty miles from Bugville. Beyond that river is a railroad track. The first town which appears to the left should be Prune City.
>
> Wonder what a pilot thinks about? Well, something very much like that as he flies over unknown territory.[34]

Earhart's passion for flying was made evident as she stated, "All I wished to do in the world was to be a vagabond—in the air."

Earhart later briefly described the early part of the flight to California: "The first stage of my hobo journey took me to Pittsburgh, Dayton, Terre Haute, St. Louis, Muskogee, and on into New Mexico."[35] She made no mention of her accident in Pittsburgh. Upon landing there, her Avro passed over a narrow ditch that was covered by grass. Her plane did a ground loop, much as a car spins out of control in an accident, damaging the propeller, lower wing, and landing gear. Putnam promptly ordered a duplicate plane to be flown from New York to Pittsburgh, so that its parts could replace the damaged parts of her plane.

Hazardous Conditions

As she was crossing Texas, Earhart flew into some bumpy weather. The gusty winds bounced her Avro so vigorously that the map pinned to her dress blew out of the open cockpit. Not seeing any landmarks, she followed a line of cars on the highway into New Mexico. Instead of heading into a town, as she had hoped, the cars veered off to their houses. Darkness was approaching, and the plane's gas was low. Seeing a village around an oil well, she landed on the dirt main street and rolled through the center of town. Earhart described the reaction of the local people:

> At once the community turned out to see who was in the plane and I turned out to see where I was. My friendly metropolis [Hobbs, New Mexico] claimed the age of six months, and the title of an oil boom town.

The citizens helped me fold the wings of the biplane and then, after sending telegrams by way of the single telephone, I dined at the Owl Cafe, from the much appreciated but invariable menu of fried eggs, coffee and bread. And the luxury of a real bed![36]

The next morning Earhart resumed her flight and in a few days landed in Glendale, California. She saw the National Air Races, talked with old acquaintances, and visited her father. Wherever Earhart went, fans and reporters followed her. When Putnam saw her pictures in a paper in New York, he wrote her, "Your hats! They are a public menace! But I hasten to add the Pittsburgh bonnet is a peach."[37] Earhart rarely wore a hat after that reproof.

Near the end of September 1928 Earhart took off for New York. Engine trouble over Utah forced her to land in a rough field, and the plane was damaged. Repairs delayed her arrival in New York until the middle of October. To her surprise, she learned that she was the first woman to complete a solo round-trip transcontinental flight.

Trials of Being a Celebrity

While Earhart was away, Putnam had been busy. He had set up her first product endorsement—for cigarettes. Since she did not smoke, she at first refused the offer. Then Putnam persuaded her to accept it because Bill Stultz and Slim Gordon, who were also to be in the advertisement, wanted the money. And she could give the fifteen hundred dollars to charity. She agreed and gave the money to Commander Byrd to help finance his next expedition.

Earhart featured in the controversial cigarette ads that her manager, Putnam, had set up for her. Earhart herself did not smoke, and the ads generated unfavorable publicity.

Some people were rankled by her endorsing cigarettes, though. "Since you smoke, I suppose you drink also," wrote one critic. "Cigarette smoking is to be expected from any woman who cuts her hair like a man's and who wears trousers in public," wrote another.[38]

The ad also cost Earhart a job. *McCall's*, a women's magazine, canceled a contract for her to become its aviation editor. *Cosmopolitan*, not finding the ad offensive, offered her an associate editorship. She agreed to write eight articles on aviation.

Meeting Orville Wright

In her biography
Amelia Earhart,
*Doris Rich describes
Earhart's attending
the International
Civil Aeronautics
Conference in 1928:*

"G.P. [Putnam] continued to notify the press of her every move. In December she attended the International Civil Aeronautics Conference in Washington, which was followed by a celebration at Kitty Hawk, North Carolina, of the twenty-fifth anniversary of the Wright brothers' first flight. Although she was not an official delegate she was one of two hundred guests invited to go by sea on the steamer, *District of Columbia*. Three thousand others had to find their own transportation.

The celebration was plagued by fog, rain, and transportation breakdowns but when the monument at Kill Devil Hill [the slope from which the Wright brothers had launched their first plane] was unveiled on December 17, Amelia was right where G.P. wanted her to be—standing between Orville Wright and Sen. Hiram Bingham, president of the NAA [National Aeronautic Association]."

Earhart and Orville Wright, two of the world's most well known pilots.

Signing the contract with *Cosmopolitan* also meant making a second commitment, as Earhart recognized:

> Ray Long, a guiding spirit of *Cosmopolitan Magazine*, asked me to join its staff as Aviation Editor. With "*Cosmo's*" enormous circulation I welcomed the opportunity to reach a great audience with my favorite subject. And in deciding to accept Mr. Long's offer, I knew that I was casting my lot permanently with aviation.[39]

In the future she would serve on Denison House's board of directors, but she had ended her career as a social worker.

For *Cosmopolitan* Earhart wrote articles such as "Try Flying Yourself," "Is It Safe for You to Fly?" and "Why Are Women Afraid to Fly?" In her articles she discussed airport services, different kinds of planes, pilot qualifications, and related topics. Underlying her comments about the safety of flying ran her constant theme—women could do anything men could do, including riding in and piloting planes. Besides writing the articles, Earhart answered many fan letters that asked questions about flying.

Getting on the Lecture Merry-Go-Round

Before sending Earhart on her first lecture tour, Putnam coached her on stage presence. According to author Doris Rich in her biography of Earhart, "He taught her how to talk into a microphone, to point at a screen without turning her back to the audience, and to avoid lowering her voice at the end of a sentence. He also advised her on posing for photographers."[40]

He instructed her to stand on the far right as she faced the camera in group pictures, so that her name would appear first in the identification under the picture. Since a gap separated her two front teeth, Putnam suggested that she smile with her mouth closed. Earhart herself must have long ago realized that the gap was not attractive, because in most of her childhood pictures she was already smiling with her lips together. "He approved of her 'natural' hair style, so artfully bleached and curled, so carefully disarranged, and of her posture, her expressive hands, and her low-pitched musical voice," Rich added.[41] Between her training at the Ogontz School and Put-

Earhart in 1929. At this time she was becoming a well-known and well-paid speaker and had also accepted a public relations job with an airline. At a time when flying was not well accepted, Earhart was supposed to convince women that commercial flying was safe and comfortable.

nam, Earhart soon faced cameras and audiences with poise.

As 1928 ended, Earhart was living in New York City in a small apartment that she rarely saw. She was rushing from one city to another, usually staying only one day, lecturing at a luncheon and often to a second group in the evening. Colleges, universities, civic organizations, and clubs all wanted to hear Earhart. After lecturing on the appeal and the safety of flying, she would answer questions about the *Friendship* flight. Her replies often included her conviction that women should become involved in flying.

Earhart's introduction to a celebrity's life in the last half of 1928 was her initiation into a completely different lifestyle. Biographer Doris Rich wrote, "She was on her way to becoming a star of the nation's lecture circuit, the principal means by which celebrities could be seen before the advent of television."[42]

In 1929 Earhart expanded her activities to aid the development of a new commercial airline. She also began speaking about women's educational opportunities, social justice, and world peace—all subjects that were important to her. Although not physically robust, Earhart maintained

The Toll of the Lectures

In Still Missing *author Susan Ware discusses the price Earhart paid for being a popular lecturer:*

"It is ironic that this world-famous aviator spent more time on the ground talking about flying than in the air, where she wanted to be. Luckily she did not mind public speaking. But she never craved the public stature of a celebrity. She merely wanted what celebrity made possible. Fellow aviator Fay Gillis Wells confirmed that her friend had no compulsion to be the center of attention: 'Some people exhibit an aura of charisma; a brilliance lights up, and bells ring—they are center stage. Amelia wasn't like that. She didn't mind the recognition, when it was earned, but she didn't want to be on stage unless it was essential to reach her goal. If it was money she needed, she would lecture her heart out to get the dues to pay the bills.'

The remarkable thing, of course, was how Amelia Earhart managed to conceal from each audience any of the strain, boredom, or stress that had gotten her to that particular podium on that particular day in Anywhere, U.S.A."

a hectic schedule as she juggled her various obligations.

Earhart's popularity as a speaker soared. By 1929 she was averaging twenty-four hundred dollars a week for her lectures. In addition she was still endorsing products, writing her column for *Cosmopolitan,* and receiving royalties from her book. When she had fulfilled the terms of her contract with the magazine, she did not renew it. She could not spare the time to write more articles.

Earhart was traveling so much that she rarely got to Medford to see her mother and her sister. On March 7 she wrote her mother a letter that would set the pattern for most of her subsequent letters to her family; it began with an apology: "Dear Mammy, Today's your birthday. I'm sorry I had to be away. Anyway I bring a sprize when I return."[43] Earhart's attempts at humor were supposed to ease the blow of disappointment.

Earhart Pioneers Commercial Aviation

Instead of setting aside time for her family and her friends, Earhart took on a job that would make her busier than ever. In the spring of 1929 businessman Clement M. Keyes was planning a transcontinental air passenger and mail service that would work with the Pennsylvania and Sante Fe Railroads. He offered Earhart the position of assistant to the general traffic manager of his new airline, Transcontinental Air Transport (TAT), later to become Trans World Airlines (TWA). Her assignment was to persuade women that flying was safe, comfortable, and convenient, not only for their husbands but for themselves as well.

Earhart interrupted her work long enough to be maid of honor at her sister's wedding to Albert Morrissey on June 29, although she missed the rehearsal and the prenuptial dinner. Fog had delayed her takeoff. Then when the sky finally cleared, she discovered that the propeller of her plane had been chipped. Rather than wait for a replacement, she took the train and arrived in time for the ceremony. After the wedding the minister talked with Earhart about the *Friendship* flight. She told him, "I think what Pidge has done today took more courage than my flying did."[44]

Back at work she learned that the chief technical adviser for the new airline would be Charles Lindbergh. Both he and Earhart were featured in the initial run on July 7, 1929. Lindbergh flew the first TAT plane from Glendale, California, to Winslow, Arizona. Earhart, traveling with passengers by plane during the day and by train during the night because night flying was not safe, landed in Winslow to join Lindbergh and his bride, Anne, on a return flight to Glendale.

On seeing Lindbergh and Earhart together, reporters resurrected the nickname Lady Lindy, much to Earhart's embarrassment. She finally wrote a letter of apology to Anne Morrow Lindbergh: "I believe I have never apologized so widely and so consistently for anything in my life. You understand my dislike of the title isn't because I don't appreciate being compared to one who has abilities such as Colonel Lindbergh has, but because the comparison is quite unjustified."[45] Reporters and fans continued to call Earhart Lady Lindy, but she never used the nickname to promote her own interests.

Earhart Enters Women's Air Derby

Between her work at TAT and the lectures Putnam was scheduling for her, Earhart was convincing more people to fly—and being paid well for her efforts. She was not, however, finding much time to fly for pleasure.

She decided to enter the first annual Women's Transcontinental Air Derby, which would inaugurate the air races at Cleveland in August. Although the women's flight had been considered as transcontinental from the beginning, the all-male committee of the sponsoring agency, the National Air Races, suddenly decided that such a long flight over the Rockies was too arduous for female pilots. The women should either fly from California to Cleveland with a navigator on board or perhaps they should fly just from Omaha to Cleveland.

Earhart reacted immediately. She notified the contest committee, the National Air Races committee, and the press that those restrictions were ridiculous. She would either fly solo from California to Cleveland, or she would not enter the race. Lady Mary Heath, Louise Thaden, and Elinor Smith were among the pilots who supported her. The committee backed down. Earhart signed up for the race on her thirty-second birthday.

Knowing that her Avro was not fast enough to win the derby, Earhart sold the small plane and bought a secondhand Lockheed Vega, a more powerful plane. When Earhart took her Vega for a checkup at the Lockheed plant in California, test pilot Wiley Post deemed the plane mechanically unfit to fly. Lockheed, which would score a real publicity advantage if both Lindbergh and Earhart, America's two premier pilots, were flying Lockheeds, offered to exchange another used Vega for her unsafe plane. She accepted the deal.

Earhart with her Lockheed Vega, the plane she flew in the Women's Transcontinental Air Derby. Lockheed gave her this plane after deeming the first one she bought unfit to fly.

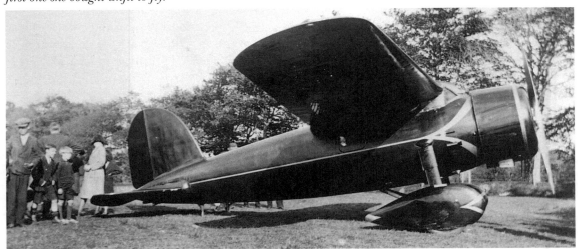

Earhart Meets the Lindberghs

Anne Morrow Lindbergh describes her first meeting with Earhart in her book Hour of Gold, Hour of Lead:

"The biggest surprise, though, was Amelia Earhart, who was here the first four days. She is the most amazing person—just as tremendous as C., [Charles], I think. It startles me how much alike they are in breadth. C. doesn't realize it, but he hasn't talked to her as much. She has the clarity of mind, impersonal eye, coolness of temperament, balance of a scientist. Aside from that, I like her."

Earhart with Anne Morrow Lindbergh, Charles Lindbergh's wife, who would later become a pilot herself.

Earhart liked to see how fast she could get from one place to another, but she was not enthusiastic about air racing. She lacked a really competitive spirit. She wanted to fly in the Women's Air Derby, however, because the race was the first real test of women as competitive pilots. Despite not having flown the Vega enough to become thoroughly familiar with it, she lined up her plane with the rest of the women's planes on August 18, 1929.

Twenty women pilots who met the requirements—an aviation license and at least a hundred hours of flying experience—were to fly from Santa Monica, California, to Cleveland, Ohio, on a prescribed course. They would fly during the day and rest at night. Whoever landed first in Cleveland on the eighth day would win. Because Earhart's Vega was the most powerful and the fastest plane entered, she was expected to win.

Master of ceremonies for the takeoff before twenty thousand spectators was Will Rogers, popular humorist, columnist, and movie star. Dubbing the race the Powder Puff Derby, he referred to the women pilots as "ladybirds" and "flying flappers."

Taking off at one-minute intervals, the pilots flew to San Bernardino, where they stayed the first night. Some of the fliers had problems along the way, and Marvel

Participants in the 1929 Women's Transcontinental Air Derby. Earhart lost her bid to win the race when she stopped to help pull another pilot out of her crashed plane. Embarrassed by her rough landings, Putnam told the press that something was wrong with Earhart's Vega.

Crossen, a bush pilot from Alaska, was killed when she had to bail out at too low an altitude. On the second day Earhart and Ruth Nichols were ahead in the race, but Nichols crashed on takeoff. Earhart stopped her Vega and ran over to help pull Nichols out of the plane—and lost her turn to take off. Everyone thought that she could make up the lost time, but Louise Thaden flew into Cleveland first and Gladys O'Donnell second. Earhart came in third.

Due to various mishaps, only eleven finished the grueling race. The major weaknesses were the undependability of the 1929 planes and the primitive navigational systems, not the frailty of the women. The "powder puffers," as even Earhart eventually called them, had proved that they were worthy of being taken seriously.

Not everyone was favorably impressed with Earhart's flying, though. The Vega came down at a faster landing speed than her smaller plane had, and her landings had been bumpy. She also had a couple of near crashes during the race. Putnam issued a statement claiming that her Vega had not been properly tuned at the factory. Earhart did not contradict his excuses. Within a few weeks, however, she did trade her plane for another second-hand Vega.

Organizing the Ninety-Nines

Early in November 1929 Earhart met at Curtiss-Wright Field on Long Island, New York, with some other fliers to form an association of women pilots. While they were considering a name for the group, Earhart suggested that it be called by the number of members. By the time they met again in February 1930, ninety-nine women pilots had paid their one-dollar membership fee, so the group called themselves the Ninety-Nines. They elected Earhart their first president. Their constitution states the club's purpose: "We propose to assist women in aeronautical research, air racing events, acquisition of aerial experience, administration of aid through aerial means in times of emergency arising from fire, famine, flood, or war."[46]

Earhart helped members of the Ninety-Nines whenever and however she could. She defended Helen Richey, first woman pilot for a commercial airline, who was fired because she had not joined the pilots union, which the all-male members would not let her join. Earhart loaned another Ninety-Niner the money to start a new business. And she quietly paid the cost of six months of treatment for alcoholism for the husband of another Ninety-Niner.

More Honors

Doris Rich, in Amelia Earhart, *describes Earhart's reception in California in September 1929:*

"The National Air Exhibition at Mines Field in Los Angeles was in its fifth day when Amelia showed up after a night's sleep at the Biltmore Hotel. This annual event was aviation's 'Barnum and Bailey Show of Shows' with crowds of fifty to seventy-five thousand attending daily to watch the world's best aviators perform. When Amelia was introduced from the announcers' stand, she received a standing ovation. Two days later, Hollywood columnist Louella Parsons wrote that a movie company filming the aviation show failed to attract the attention of spectators who were more interested in getting 'a glimpse of Colonel Lindbergh and Amelia Earhart.'

That same week Amelia flew as a passenger to San Francisco, where she paid a visit to the Army's 381st Aero Squadron at Cressey Field. The squadron made her an honorary major and presented her with the silver pilot's wings of the U.S. Air Service. She obviously prized this gift more than any other she had received and wore the wings frequently for the rest of her life—even on formal gowns."

Although Earhart gained fame in the late 1920s largely due to the publicity efforts of her manager, she had less and less time for the thing she became famous for—flying.

Earhart Sets Speed Records

On November 22, 1929, Earhart set a women's speed record over a designated course by averaging 184.19 miles an hour over four laps. The National Aeronautic Association refused to recognize Earhart's record, even though it had been timed by an official from the NAA, because the organization had a category for a one-mile straightaway course only for men. Earhart spent the next eight months badgering the NAA to set up categories for women, even if temporarily. She flew two trials on

June 25, 1930, and a third on July 5 and set three new records for women: one hundred kilometers at 174.897 miles an hour; one hundred kilometers with a load of five hundred kilograms at 171.438 miles an hour; and three kilometers at 181.18 miles an hour. After haggling with the NAA for another year, she finally was recognized by the Federation Aeronautique Internationale for her world records.

Earhart had planned to spend Christmas of 1929 with Amy and Muriel, who was now pregnant with her first child. On December 18, however, Amelia wrote her mother from Los Angeles:

> Dear Mammy,
>   Hooray for Chrizmuzz. Here's something for you and Pidge. I can't make it in time I think, but will probably arrive for a while shortly after.
>   How's Pidge? I hope she's feeling better.
>   Let me know when you are short and I'll send along some cash.
>   Goo' bye [47]

The year 1929 had been an especially busy one for Earhart—lecturing, working for TAT, meeting the Lindberghs, buying a bigger plane, flying in the Women's Air Derby, helping to organize the Ninety-Nines. She had written only brief notes to her mother and her sister, and she sometimes did not call them even when she was only minutes away in Boston.

Not only was Earhart too busy to give time to her family and her friends, but she was usually even too busy to fly for the pleasure that flying alone always gave her. Some of the other women pilots blamed her mediocre flying skills on her lack of flying time. They ultimately blamed Putnam for booking her schedule too solidly.

Chapter

5 The Marriage Cage

Early in 1930 Earhart accepted a public relations position with the Pennsylvania Railroad in addition to her work with TAT. She needed more money because she wanted to set up a permanent income for her mother, who was now living with Muriel. Amelia wrote her mother on February 3, 1930:

> Dear Mother,
> I am enclosing a check for $100. Hereafter you will receive it monthly from the Fifth Avenue Bank. I have put all of my savings into stocks and bonds and the yearly income in your name. The list includes the $1000 bond of yours which you may have, of course, at any time. I also have you down as beneficiary of a small fraternal endowment which you will receive in case I pop off.
> I plan to work hard this year and [do] little else but fly.[48]

And work she did. In February she flew in an exhibition in St. Louis with Frank Hawks, Elinor Smith, and Jimmy Doolittle, among others. In April she watched maneuvers from the aircraft carrier *Lexington* with assistant secretaries of the navy and commerce departments and several members of the U.S. Congress. Putnam wanted her to appear at such af-

fairs so that she would continue to appeal as a speaker. In April, May, and June she flew from one town to another to address civic groups.

Earhart in 1930. Earhart worked hard both to keep her name in the public eye as manager George Putnam wanted, and to support her mother.

Earhart Joins New Air Shuttle Service

And she associated herself with another airline. While working for TAT, Earhart had become acquainted with Paul Collins, superintendent of operations, and Gene Vidal, an engineer on the technical staff. Those two seasoned pilots wanted to pioneer a new kind of airline, a shuttle service from New York City to Washington, D.C. Collins and Vidal left the security of TAT in the spring of 1930 to seek financial backing and to prepare a detailed cost analysis and operational plan. Since financiers Charles and Nicholas Ludington were their backers, Collins and Vidal named their service the Ludington Line. They invited Earhart to be vice president of public relations. According to her, "It was to be an hourly service with ten round trips a day, the first of its kind ever attempted over such a distance."[49] A flight from New York to Washington cost twenty dollars. The flights were an immediate success.

As with TAT, Earhart supervised passenger services. She was to attract customers with her speeches, to satisfy any passenger concern, and to quell their fears and misgivings. She described her speaking tour: "During this period of vocal salesmanship, I met college girls, women's clubs, and professional groups and mixtures of these, as well as all sorts and conditions of men before whom I also spoke."[50]

Family Problems

Not only did Earhart miss visiting her mother on her birthday again in 1930, but her gifts were late as well. In May Earhart ended a brief letter to her mother, "I'll try to get up there as soon as I can for a short visit, though I can't say definitely when that will be."[51] Another time Earhart began a letter to her mother, "I am sorry I haven't answered your letter before, but I have been and am terribly occupied with the infant airline."[52]

Earhart interrupted her frantic schedule late in September 1930 because her father's health had deteriorated, and he lay near death. She flew to Los Angeles and spent almost a week with him and his second wife, Helen. When he appeared to be improving, Amelia started to fly back. Helen's wire caught her at Tucson: Edwin had died about eight hours after Amelia's

Amelia visited her father in 1930 when she learned that he was gravely ill. Once it seemed he had improved, Earhart left, only to receive news that her father had died shortly thereafter.

departure. She wrote her mother, "He asked about you and Pidge a lot, and I faked telegrams for him from you all. He was an aristocrat as he went."[53]

Putnam Makes a Proposal

One reason that Earhart stepped up her schedule in 1930 was that Putnam had more time to devote to her career. He and his wife had divorced in December 1929. Earhart and Putnam were often together as they planned her projects, and he sometimes accompanied her on her lecture tours. When they were in New York, they attended plays and parties together. Most of their acquaintances assumed that they would marry. Putnam did, too, and he proposed five times, but she always refused. She still believed that marriage would be too confining and that it would curtail her flying. As she was preparing to leave for another lecture, he proposed for the sixth time. She patted his arm, said "Yes," climbed into her Vega, and took off. Her cavalier, or offhand, response to his proposal would characterize her attitude toward their marrying.

Why did Earhart—at age thirty-three—finally decide to marry? After all, the marriage she had observed most closely, her parents', had ended in divorce. And as far as Amelia could see, Muriel was struggling with an unhappy marriage.

Earhart had long described marriage as a cage. She wanted to be free to take off in her plane whenever she felt like doing so. For her, keeping house and rearing children were confining drudgeries. Too, she had been the acting head of her family since she was fourteen, and she knew that

Once Putnam (left) divorced his wife in 1929, he and Earhart spent all of their time together at work as well as play, attending concerts, plays, and parties.

she would always have to help support her mother and Muriel and help them make decisions. She would continue to live her own life apart from theirs, but she would willingly provide for them financially.

Amelia knew that her mother did not approve of Putnam: he was ten years older than Amelia, and he was divorced. Since Amy was also divorced, her second objection was hardly persuasive. Muriel, who had barely met Putnam, was awed by him.

Possibly one of the most important reasons for not marrying was Earhart's need to be her private self now and then. Before her audiences she wore her public

Earhart and Putnam pose for the camera. After being asked many times by Putnam to marry him, Earhart finally agreed at the age of thirty-three.

figure mask: composed, confident, courageous. Before Amy and Muriel she wore her family mask: an authoritative air softened by affection and generosity. Between her family, her many acquaintances, and her few friends and herself she maintained an invisible, impenetrable wall. She had always hidden her private self from others. In a marriage, would she have room to hide?

On the other hand, the Great Depression was getting worse not only in the United States, but all over the world. Flying was an expensive hobby, even in good times. Although Earhart was making good money, she could not afford to buy new planes or to finance long flights. Putnam had managed her career ever since the *Friendship* flight. Furthermore, they had several common interests. They both enjoyed plays, concerts, adventures, reading, and the same kind of people. Finally, she had emphasized in her lectures that women should combine careers with their marriages. She could prove that she was right.

Putnam came from a background far different from Earhart's. Born to wealth, he had always circulated among the social elite. As an editor at his grandfather's publishing house, G.P. Putnam's Sons, he was best known for procuring the books of famous explorers and adventurers—Rear Admiral Richard Byrd, Roy Chapman Andrews, Martin and Osa Johnson, Charles Lindbergh, and most recently, Earhart. Putnam himself had led two scientific expeditions—one to Greenland, one to Baffin Island. He had also written a book about the ill-fated balloon flight of the Swedish explorer Salomon August Andrée to the North Pole. When the book came out in October 1930, Putnam had dedicated it "To a favorite aeronaut."

Putnam knew many celebrities, but few called him a friend. According to author Gore Vidal (son of Gene Vidal, Earhart's coworker at TAT and at the shuttle service) in a Public Broadcasting System documentary about Earhart, "I never knew anybody who liked George Palmer Putnam. Everybody who knew him disliked him." On the same program Earhart biographer Doris Rich added, "He was a super editor and a better publicist. He could be enormously charming and be totally insulting at times. His language ranged from the erudite [scholarly] to really ugly profanity. He was a very complex, driven man."[54]

The Bridegroom

In his biography Winged Legend: The Story of Amelia Earhart, *John Burke defends George Palmer Putnam as a good match for Earhart:*

"The man who marries a celebrity and intends to be a husband as well as a luggage-bearing consort requires a resilient ego and a large amount of self-confidence. It helps considerably if he is successful in his own right. Even more if he is a man of affairs able and willing to spare the time to manage his wife's career.

George Palmer Putnam figured that he fulfilled the requirements. He was a hard-driving, ambitious fellow with the habit of command. Rimless glasses may have given him the appearance of a sedate professor of history, but he was a man of action who possessed a strongly competitive urge and hated to lose out in anything. He had attended Harvard and the University of California at Berkeley, cut himself loose from his wealthy family with $300 in his pocket, and announced his determination to achieve success on his own. Within a few years he was not only the editor of the local newspaper but mayor of Bend, Oregon."

Putnam was aggressive, abrasive, and insensitive to the feelings of others. Although he had considerable management skills, his tactics were sometimes ruthless. Elinor Smith, a pilot younger than Earhart, believed that Putnam had prevented her from receiving publicity and product endorsements—both of which she desperately needed—because he considered her a threat to Earhart's success. Reporters soon learned that they would have to listen to Putnam for fifteen or twenty minutes before they could talk with Earhart. Most people who liked Earhart tolerated him for her sake.

Why Should They Marry?

Why would this dissimilar pair want to marry? Each had something the other craved. Earhart wanted to fly, and she wanted to set records. She had done little yet to earn the celebrity status she enjoyed. Most of the other women pilots were borrowing or begging money to finance their flights. Putnam, the consummate promoter and manager, could get her planes and the funds to finance the flights she wanted to make. Putnam, on the other hand, moved among celebrities, but he himself was not the celebrity he yearned to be. To achieve their goals, they needed each other.

On November 8, 1930, Putnam got a marriage license in Noank, Connecticut, where his mother lived. He arranged for a judge and the town clerk to bring the license to Mrs. Putnam's home for Earhart to sign. Thereafter the news media hounded the couple more closely than ever, but for the next few weeks the pair kept saying that they had not set a date. On February 4, 1931, Earhart wrote her mother :

Earhart and Putnam one year after their marriage in 1932. Earhart, unconventional as ever, handed Putnam a marriage contract that stated he would not interfere in her life. She also refused to wear a wedding band.

Earhart Was Not Sold on Marriage

Putnam knew that Earhart had real doubts about marriage. In Soaring Wings *he quotes from a letter she had written to a friend in 1930:*

"'I am still unsold on marriage. I don't want *anything* all of the time. A den. . . . Do you remember in "If Winter Comes" how Mabel was always trying to get her husband a "den," and how he hated it. He said he wasn't a bear. A den is stuffy. I'd rather live in a tree.

I think I may not ever be able to see marriage except as a cage until I am unfit to work or fly or be active—and of course I wouldn't be desirable then.'

In her heart she knew that, for good or ill, she must keep freedom in a measure which is not always possible in marriage. She had no selfish dream of the anatomy of freedom, but she did know it for an element without which she personally could not do, as some plants can do without water, but cannot survive without air."

Dear Momie,

I shant be home over this next weekend. Why don't you plan your trip for next one? Of course if you wish, come anyway, and Nora [her secretary] can attend details of room, etc.

I am due in Wash. tonight and have a luncheon in Newark today.

Cheerio,
A.[55]

The Wedding

Three days later, on Saturday, February 7 —without even a hint to her mother— Earhart married Putnam at his mother's home. Just before the ceremony began, Earhart handed Putnam a letter that was basically a marriage contract. Especially noteworthy are four conditions of her letter. She did not expect either of them to give up any phase of their lives before their marriage. She asked for no concessions, nor did she grant any. She insisted that they keep their private lives private. She asked that he release her at the end of the year if they did not find life together congenial. Putnam agreed to Earhart's terms.

The wedding was more remarkable for what did not happen than for what did. She had not invited any member of her family. The word *obey* was not included in the vows. She did not assume her groom's name, then or ever. Instead of bridal finery, she wore a familiar brown suit and brown shoes. Earhart took off the wedding ring after the ceremony and never wore it again.

Witnesses to the marriage were Putnam's mother, the judge who performed the ceremony, his son, who was Mrs. Putnam's lawyer, and two black cats. After the couple had exchanged their vows, the bride resumed her conversation with the lawyer about a new kind of plane, the autogiro. Then the newlyweds left for an undisclosed destination—but not before Putnam had called his secretary to notify the press. Earhart wired Muriel: "Over the broomstick with GP [Putnam] today. Break the news gently to Mother."[56] Each was back at work Monday morning.

Both were engrossed in their own careers, as well as in their joint projects. After selling his shares in the publishing company, Putnam became an editorial director for Paramount Pictures, a job that gave him more time to manage Earhart's career. Earhart needed to make more money after her marriage than she had before. She and Putnam shared their living expenses equally, while she continued to support her mother regularly and to help Muriel occasionally. She was also sending some money to an ill cousin and to an uncle.

Family Problems

Soon after Earhart's wedding, she arranged a twenty-five-hundred-dollar loan to Muriel and Albert for a down payment on a house. As usual, Amelia was willing to help, especially since her mother now lived with Muriel and her family. However, Amelia wanted the loan set up as a business transaction—a request that Muriel failed to acknowledge. Finally Amelia wrote a reminder to her mother:

Please have Muriel send me a properly drawn second mortgage. I suppose it is impossible to impress upon her the

fact that [a] businesslike relationship between relatives is not an unfriendly act. I'm no Scrooge to ask that some acknowledgement of a twenty-five hundred dollar loan be given me. I work hard for my money. Whether or not I shall expect payment is my business.[57]

To keep money coming in, Earhart needed to become newsworthy again. Some of her flying records had been broken. Elinor Smith had set a new altitude record; Ruth Nichols broke Smith's record and then Earhart's speed record. Earhart's ride across the Atlantic was her only claim to fame, and that event had happened almost three years earlier.

Near the end of 1930 Earhart had flown an autogiro, the forerunner of the helicopter. Putnam quickly saw the autogiro as the vehicle to bolster Earhart's fame, since no other woman had flown that kind of aircraft. She flew one to a new altitude record—18,451 feet—on April 8, 1931. Her flight was not officially recorded, but it brought her favorable publicity nevertheless.

In May she bought a Pitcairn autogiro so that she could be the first person to fly an autogiro across the continent. Seeking a sponsor, Putnam sold the plane to the Beech-Nut gum company, which promptly painted "BEECH-NUT" in large letters on the body of the "flying windmill" and then lent it to Earhart for the transcontinental flight. She reached Los Angeles on June 7, only to learn that a pilot named Johnny Miller had beaten her by one week. According to biographer Mary Lovell, "Amelia was disappointed and George was furious."[58]

Earhart tried to salvage the trip by flying a different first—a round-trip transcontinental flight in an autogiro. On the way back she stopped at Abilene, Texas, to take part in an air fair. After demonstrating the plane and taking some people up for rides, Earhart and her mechanic lifted up to resume their journey. They had risen just a few feet when one of the rotors caught a landing light. In the ensuing crash, some of the falling debris hit some of the spectators and damaged some cars. When the Department of Commerce reprimanded her for being "careless" and

"using bad judgment," Earhart brushed the criticisms aside: "We'd have made it but for the crowd. The air just went out from under me at 30 or 50 feet up— maybe one of those hot little whirlwinds did it. I was afraid a child might run out suddenly or we might hit a car. Both crowds and cars were parked too closely infield. I did what I thought was best in the circumstances."[59]

Earhart had a second experience with an autogiro in September 1931, when

Putnam and Earhart pose before the autogiro she would fly across the continent. Putnam arranged to have the Beech-Nut company sponsor the flight.

Beech-Nut sent her to Detroit on another promotional flight. Putnam accompanied her, as he often did. While she was flying the autogiro to the park in the state fair grounds, Putnam stood nearby talking to a spectator. A sudden crashing sound halted the conversation. Putnam jumped over the rail and ran toward the fallen autogiro. He described his reaction in *Soaring Wings:* "Never have I run so fast—until one of those guy wires caught my pumping legs exactly at the ankles. I did a complete outside loop, up into the air and over, landing full on my back. Crack!" Earhart climbed out of the plane and ran over to help her husband. "So flying is the safest—after all!" Earhart grinned. "If you'd been with me, you wouldn't have been hurt."[60]

Product Endorsements

To increase Earhart's income, Putnam negotiated several other product endorsements for her. She signed her name to a

---

The Marriage Contract

Nowhere does Earhart show so much her reluctance to marry as she does in the marriage contract she asked Putnam to accept. Susan Ware quotes the contract in Still Missing:

"You must know again my reluctance to marry, my feeling that I shatter thereby chances in work which mean much to me. I feel the move just now as foolish as anything I could do. I know there may be compensations, but have no heart to look ahead.

On our life together I want you to understand I shall not hold you to any medieval code of faithfulness to me, nor shall I consider myself bound to you similarly. If we can be honest I think the difficulties which may arise may best be avoided should you or I become interested deeply (or in passing) with anyone else.

Please let us not interfere with the other's work or play, nor let the world see our private joys or disagreements. In this connection I may have to keep some place where I can go to be myself now and then, for I cannot guarantee to endure at all times the confinement of even an attractive cage.

I must exact a cruel promise, and that is you will let me go in a year if we find no happiness together.

I will try to do my best in every way and give you that part of me you know and seem to want."

---

line of stationery, a set of luggage, and flight jackets. Using some principles of airplane structure, she helped design the luggage and made it lighter but more durable.

Putnam thought he had another good seller when he contracted with a clothing manufacturer to produce a copy of the hat Earhart had worn when she landed in America after the *Friendship* flight. The hat, which would be decorated with a band bearing her name, would cost fifty cents to make and would sell to children for three dollars. When Earhart heard of the plan, she adamantly refused to approve it and ordered Putnam to cancel the contract. She would not cheat children. Ordinarily, though, she went along with his schemes.

Earhart did need to keep money coming in, for her mother required continuing assistance. When Amy suggested that she pay room and board to Muriel and Albert, Amelia fired off a letter to her mother:

I am very much displeased at the use you have put what I hoped you would save. I am not working to help Albert, nor Pidge much as I care for her.

I do not mean to be harsh, but I know the family failing about money. As for your paying board, such a thing is unthinkable as you have done all the housekeeping which more than compensates. It is true that I have a home and food but what I send you is what I myself earn and it does not come from GP [Putnam].[61]

Earhart's home was the spacious Putnam house in Rye, New York. Occasionally she would briefly play at housekeeping when she would consult with the housekeeper about some minor household matter. She did like to work in the flower

Earhart with her stepson David Putnam in 1932. Although certainly not a typical stepmother, Earhart tried to entertain George Putnam's sons whenever they visited the couple.

garden. Whenever Putnam's sons came for a visit, Earhart would clear her appointment book so that she could entertain them.

Amelia kept promising to bring Amy to Rye for a visit but somehow did not get around to doing it. Muriel, who had decided to make the best of a bad marriage, was totally involved with her family, her church, and her teaching. Biographer Jean Backus evaluated the relationship of the three women:

Both women loved Amelia, delighted in her rare visits, and relied on her for advice and financial aid as they would

Analysis of the Marriage Contract

Ware studies the implications of Earhart's marriage contract in Still Missing:

"The letter [contract] expressed a deep-seated fear that marriage would destroy her chances of productive work. Other women entered marriage blinded by passion or radiant about the future; Amelia seemed practically immobilized (she had 'no heart to look ahead') and could only hope that it wouldn't be as bad as she feared. She expressed her deep need to maintain her own sense of self with her Virginia Woolf-like request 'to keep some place where I can go to be myself.' (Note the phrase said 'be myself,' not 'be by myself.') Her choice of the words 'confinement' and 'cage' to describe the institution of marriage are especially telling. In fact, she was so unsure about the outcome that she bound Putnam to the 'cruel promise' of letting her go in a year if they were unhappy."

have relied on the man of the family. But the news stories they read about her and the questions they were asked about her and about themselves were alien in their world, and in hers they were strangers and ill at ease.[62]

Earhart Writes a Second Book

Earhart spent the last few weeks of 1931 working on her second book, *The Fun of It.* The first two-thirds of the book covers her life up to 1931, as well as general topics about aviation. In the final third she describes the feats of some of the other pioneer women pilots. She does not mention her husband until the last chapter, in which she discusses the project she was planning for 1932.

As 1931 ended, Earhart had managed to stay in the public eye as an immensely popular figure, thanks mostly to her husband's efforts. She had helped to advance the development of commercial aviation, but she certainly had scored no major personal triumph that would anchor her position as America's premier woman pilot. She did have in mind, however, a flight that would realize that goal.

6 Having to Be First

On January 1, 1932, Earhart had been living in her marriage cage almost a year. No evidence suggests that either she or Putnam ever took advantage of the freedom she had offered in her marriage contract. On February 7 she did not ask to be released from their marriage. Instead, with her husband doubling as her manager, she would concentrate on flying. Although she still wanted to earn some of the acclaim showered on her after the *Friendship* flight, she also wanted to prove that female pilots were fully as competent as male pilots. If she could prove that she was a competent flier, she could lead the way for other women fliers. As a means of proving her point, she elected to set more records in flying.

As usual Earhart thought her first project through before she disclosed the details to anyone—even to Putnam. In *Soaring Wings* he remembered when she had told him of her plan:

> For as the calendar rolled into 1932 AE told me she felt ready to fly the Atlantic alone. I must have known for four years really that she wanted to.
>
> We talked of it from time to time, but always casually. But I remember one morning that AE lowered her morning newspaper for one moment

and said slowly "Would you *mind* if I flew the Atlantic?"[63]

Earhart later clarified her reasons for making the transatlantic flight: "It was clear in my mind that I was undertaking the flight for the fun of it. I chose to fly the Atlantic because I wanted to. It was, in a measure, a self-justification—a proving to me, and to anyone else interested, that a woman with adequate experience could do it."[64] Those two reasons she would give for every record-setting flight of her career.

Since Lindbergh's flight, only crews—including that of the *Friendship*—had flown the Atlantic. Not only had no individuals—men or women—flown it, but Lady Mary Heath had publicly proclaimed that women would not be ready to fly the Atlantic for at least ten years.

"You Can Do It"

Earhart and Putnam invited Bernt Balchen, pilot for Commander Byrd, to lunch in Rye to discuss her plan. While they were playing croquet after lunch, Earhart told Balchen that she wanted to fly the Atlantic solo. Then she asked him three questions: "Am I ready to do it? Is the ship ready? Will you help me?"

Balchen's answers were slow in coming, for he considered each question in turn. "You can do it. The ship—when we are through with it—will be o.k. And—I'll help." [65]

As the three planned her flight, Balchen persuaded Earhart to fly a shorter route than Lindbergh had taken. He had left from New York. If she took off from Harbour Grace, Newfoundland, she would shorten the flying time considerably, thus saving some physical strain. Reaching for maximum publicity, Putnam tentatively scheduled Earhart's flight for the fifth anniversary of Lindbergh's transatlantic flight, if weather conditions were favorable. She would aim for Paris if the flight was going smoothly; if not, she would land in Ireland.

As with her first transatlantic journey, her crew maintained secrecy. Earhart chartered her Vega to Balchen, and people assumed that he was preparing it for another expedition. In an old Fokker hangar in Teterboro, New Jersey, Balchen and Eddie Gorski, his mechanic, adapted the Vega for ocean flight. After strengthening the fuselage, they installed additional fuel tanks to give the plane a capacity of 420 gallons, enough to ensure a range of at least thirty-two hundred miles. They replaced the old engine with a new, more powerful, five-hundred horsepower Wasp engine. Although the Vega had a magnetic compass, they added two other types of compasses, as well as a drift indicator—all to make navigation more precise. Remembering how the pontoons had complicated take-offs of the *Friendship*, Earhart refused to have them installed on the Vega.

On a test flight Balchen and Gorski flew the Vega loaded with sandbags to see if it could tolerate the weight of the extra fuel. "We couldn't land with all that weight," Gorski said, "so I pushed the

Earhart in the Lockheed Vega she would use to make a solo transatlantic flight.

Earhart with Bernt Balchen, who would help prepare the Vega for Earhart's transatlantic flight.

sandbags out while Bernt flew back and forth over the Jersey meadowlands. People thought we were dropping bombs."[66]

During the early spring Earhart maintained her usual schedule of lecturing, being interviewed, and answering her extensive correspondence. She did not in any letter to her mother mention the transatlantic flight. In mid-April she began to learn to operate the new instruments in her plane. She concentrated especially on learning to fly by instruments only. Major Edwin Aldrin (father of astronaut Edwin "Buzz" Aldrin, the second man to walk on the moon) taught her how to draw fuel from the different tanks without unbalancing the weight distribution of the fuel. Doc Kimball, of the U.S. Weather Bureau in New York, again advised her about possible weather conditions on the unpredictable Atlantic.

Flying the Atlantic Solo

On May 18 in New York, Earhart christened the *Resolute*, Goodyear's new dirigible. She was at Teterboro on May 19 just before noon when Doc Kimball forecast clear weather to Harbour Grace. Racing back to Rye, she changed into her slacks, a white silk shirt, a scarf, and a leather jacket. Carrying her flight suit, a comb, a toothbrush, and a can of tomato juice, she returned to her car and drove back to Teterboro. To save Earhart's energy, Balchen flew the Vega to Newfoundland, with Earhart and Gorski on the floor behind one of the new fuel tanks. She slept most of the way. After their takeoff, Putnam called Earhart's mother and sister—and the press.

Arriving at St. John, New Brunswick, too late to go on to Harbour Grace, they

The Jewel in Her Crown

Biographer Susan Ware, in Still Missing, *rates the Atlantic solo flight among Earhart's finest:*

"Of all of Amelia Earhart's aviation accomplishments, her 1932 Atlantic solo was probably her most noteworthy and most widely praised feat. She was the first person since Lindbergh to fly the Atlantic solo, her crossing was done in record time, and she was the first person to have crossed the Atlantic by air twice. She was honored by the Distinguished Flying Cross from the U.S. Congress; the Harmon trophy; the Legion of Honor from the French government and the Gold Medal of the National Geographic Society presented by President Herbert Hoover. The presentation of the society's medal put Earhart in the elite company of the twelve men who had received the medal since 1906, including polar explorers Robert E. Peary and Roald Amundsen, Admiral Richard Byrd, and Colonel Charles Lindbergh. Ten thousand requested tickets to the National Geographic function, and thousands more listened to the live radio broadcast on NBC."

spent the night in a hotel. The next morning they flew on to Harbour Grace and arrived around 2:00, just as the fog rolled in. While Balchen and Gorski tuned the engine, Earhart took a nap. They called her at 6:00 to tell her the fog had lifted. Balchen later described her pre-flight checks and 7:12 P.M. takeoff:

> She looks at me with a small, lonely smile and says, "Do you think I can make it?" and I grin back, "You bet!"
>
> She crawls calmly into the cockpit of the big, empty airplane, starts the engine, runs it up, checks the mags [magnetos, which produce electrical spark for ignition,] and nods her

head. We pull the chocks [tire blocks] and she's off.[67]

For the first four hours the weather was so fair that Earhart enjoyed watching first the sun set, then the moon rise. She cruised at twelve thousand feet.

Troubles Began

About 11:30 P.M. Earhart began to have problems. First she saw flames through a broken weld in the manifold, or exhaust pipe. Knowing that the fire looked worse at night than it probably was, she could only hope that the metal was heavy enough to hold until she reached land. Second, the hands on the altimeter, the instrument that indicates flying height, began to spin uselessly. Then she flew into an hour-long storm whose strong winds bounced the Vega around in the sky as if it were a kite. When the storm abated, she tried to climb above the clouds, but the ascent was so slow that she knew that ice was coating the plane. At that point the tachometer, which measures the speed of the engine's revolutions, picked up ice and failed. She descended low enough to see waves so that the ice could melt at the lower temperature, but then fog engulfed her. Trying to find a middle level between the ocean and the ice, Earhart nosed through the fog. She had to rely on the gyrocompass, the most accurate of the compasses, to keep her on course.

As Earhart reported in *The Fun of It:*

Of course, the last two hours were the hardest. My exhaust manifold was vibrating very badly, and then I turned on the reserve tank and found the gauge leaking. I decided I should come down at the very nearest place, wherever it was. I had flown a set compass course all night. Now I changed to due east and headed for Ireland.[68]

New Records, New Status

After "frightening all of the cattle in the country," Earhart landed in a meadow in Londonderry, Ireland, early Saturday afternoon on May 21, 1932—fourteen hours and fifty-six minutes and 1,026.5 miles from Harbour Grace, Newfoundland.[69] On that day she set three records that would always be hers: She was the first woman to fly the Atlantic, the first woman to fly it solo, and the first person to fly it twice. The two other records she established would eventually be broken: She crossed the Atlantic in the shortest time, and she had flown the longest nonstop distance by a woman.

Earhart in Londonderry, Ireland. Upon reaching Ireland, Earhart set three records: She was the first woman to fly the Atlantic, the first woman to fly it solo, and the first woman to fly it twice.

Before her transatlantic solo, Earhart had been the best-known woman pilot in the world. In completing the treacherous flight and in handling the emergencies that occurred, she silenced some of the critics of her flying skills. And she had finally earned some of the praise that had been heaped on her after the *Friendship* flight.

Earhart herself did not voice these claims. According to Muriel, Amelia was as modest and truthful as ever:

My flight had added nothing to aviation. After all, literally hundreds have crossed the Atlantic by air if those who have gone in heavier-than-air and lighter-than-air craft are counted and those who have crossed the North and South Atlantic. However, I hope the flight has meant something to women in aviation. If it has, I shall feel it was justified; but can't claim anything else.[70]

The day after her successful crossing, cables flooded the Associated Press office in Londonderry. One message was especially poignant. It came from the Lindberghs, who were in seclusion and

Her Severest Critics

In both 1928 and 1932 caustic criticism of Earhart came from the editor of the British magazine The Aeroplane. *In 1932 an anonymous critic berated her to the president of the National Aeronautic Association, as Mary Lovell tells in* The Sound of Wings:

"'On Saturday, May 21st, Mrs. G.P. Putnam, known professionally, or for purposes of publicity, as Miss Amelia Earhart, landed at Londonderry, in or near the Irish Free State, from Harbour Grace, Newfoundland. This proves that in 1932 with a modern aeroplane, a modern engine, and the latest navigational instruments, a woman is capable of doing what a mere man did in 1919, but in three hours less than the man's time.

We cannot think why she did it, except of course for her own gratification. It does nothing for the good of aviation. And we all know that quite a number of men who are not by any means good pilots have got across the Atlantic whereas others who were remarkably good pilots have fallen in.'. . .

In a letter to the president of the NAA (Amelia was vice-president), one apparent misogynist [woman hater] wrote: 'Only an average flyer, she has pushed herself to the front by following the tactics of the feminists. Using a manmade perfect machine, tuned by men mechanics, trained by men flyers, [and a] course laid out by a man, by a lucky break she just managed to make the hop.'"

grieving for their young son who, after having been kidnapped on March 1, had been found dead on May 12. Their cable read, "We do congratulate you . . . your flight is a splendid success."[71] Ruth Nichols was a gracious loser: "You beat me to it for the second time but it was a splendid job."[72] Amy and Muriel, President Herbert Hoover, Prime Minister MacDonald on behalf of King George and Queen Mary of Great Britain, writer Fannie Hurst, and suffragist Carrie Chapman Catt were among the hundreds who sent messages of congratulation.

Since Earhart did not have Hilton Railey to manage her reception this time, she called Putnam to join her. Just before he sailed on the SS *Olympic*, he wrote a note to Amelia's mother, inviting her and Muriel to come to New York for Amelia's arrival and the planned celebration. Then he closed the letter:

> It will, I imagine, be a pretty hectic time. Likely we will be going to Washington that midnight.
>
> Of course we would love to have you. On the other hand, possibly you would prefer to keep out of the circus and come to us a little later at Rye for a quiet visit.[73]

Renewing Her World Celebrity Status

In London messages continued to arrive by the bagful. For twelve days in London Earhart was a whirlwind of activity—giving speeches and attending luncheons, teas, and receptions. When she met the Prince of Wales, later King Edward VIII, she nodded her head in greeting but did not

Charles and Anne Lindbergh found the time to congratulate Earhart on her transatlantic flight even though they were in seclusion after the kidnapping and murder of their young son.

curtsy. At a formal ball later in the week, Earhart danced with him several times.

In 1928 Earhart had been shy and apologetic and modest. In 1932 she was poised and confident and modest. In speeches she concentrated on three themes: She had flown the Atlantic for the fun of it, women were capable pilots, and

Earhart enjoys a ticker tape parade in her honor in New York after her transatlantic flight. Her reception equaled that of Charles Lindbergh's.

transatlantic commercial flights would be a reality in the near future.

On June 3 Earhart met Putnam in Cherbourg, France, and they went on to Paris by train. For five days the French people lauded her. Then the couple went on to Rome, where they were received by the pope and later by Mussolini, Italy's dictator. Then they headed for Brussels, where they dined with King Albert and the royal family and met the famous balloonist André Picard.

The American Reception

As in 1928, Earhart received criticism as well as commendation in 1932. M. E. Tracy wrote in the New York *World-Telegram*, "Amelia has given us a magnificent display of useless courage."[74] A few other American newspapers printed similar comments, but most were complimentary.

When Earhart and Putnam docked in New York in mid-June, her reception was even greater than in 1928. She was a hero in her own right this time. The ticker tape parade for her equaled the one for Lindbergh.

The next day Earhart, accompanied by Putnam and his son David, her cousin Lucy Challis, Paul Collins, and Bernt Balchen, flew to Washington. After dinner with President and Mrs. Hoover at the White House, the group went to Constitution Hall, where President Hoover presented Earhart with the National Geographic Society's Gold Medal for being the first woman to make a solo flight over the Atlantic Ocean. At a later White House ceremony she said, "I shall be happy if my small exploit has drawn attention to the fact that women are flying, too."[75]

In all of her speeches about her Atlantic solo, Earhart did not waver from her statement that she had taken the flight for fun. She defended her position forcefully:

> To want in one's heart to do a thing, for its own sake; to enjoy doing it; to concentrate all one's energies upon it—that is not only the surest guarantee of its success. It is also being true to oneself. If there is anything I have learned in life it is this: *If you follow the inner desire of your heart, the incidentals will take care of themselves.*[76]

The final banquet honoring Earhart was in Los Angeles on July 8. Hosted by

(Above) President Herbert Hoover invited Earhart to the White House to congratulate her on her transatlantic flight. (Left) Earhart waves to crowds during the parade in New York. Unlike her first transatlantic flight, Earhart felt she fully deserved the attention she received for her second one.

the National Aeronautic Association, the dinner was attended by the Ninety-Nines and colleagues from her novice pilot days. Earhart was a pilot being applauded by her fellow pilots.

A few days after the banquet Earhart headed back east for what she had intended to be a nonstop transcontinental speed record. A mechanical failure forced her down at Columbus, Ohio, and ended that attempt. She was back in Los Angeles on July 29 to accept the Distinguished Flying Cross and a congressional citation from Vice President Charles Curtis, who was in Los Angeles to open the summer Olympic Games. On her return trip to New York on August 24, Earhart flew nonstop from Los Angeles to Newark, New Jersey—the first woman to do so—in record time: nineteen hours and five minutes.

Earhart closed the year by receiving two honorary titles. In October 1932 the *Philadelphia Inquirer* reported that Earhart had been named Outstanding American Woman of the Year, a title she accepted for all women pilots. In December Earhart received an honorary doctor of science degree from Thiel College, her father's alma mater. She learned that his classmates remembered him as a bright young man with great promise of having an exciting career.

After celebrating the new year by buying a new, more powerful Vega in January 1933, Earhart needed to augment her income. Contrary to popular belief, the Putnams were not wealthy, although together they were making a lot of money. However, maintaining the house at Rye and an apartment in New York City, commuting between New York and Los Angeles, Earhart's flying, and associating with the social elite entailed expenses that left them little reserve.

Back to Work

Earhart briefly got involved in designing and selling women's clothes, but her main source of income remained her lectures. In one stretch she gave twenty-three speeches in twenty-five days at three hundred dollars a lecture. By then she was giving equal time in her lectures to aviation and women's rights. She even handed President Hoover a petition for an equal rights amendment to the U.S. Constitution. The federal government, Earhart now believed, should take the first steps toward ending discrimination against women.

In September 1934 Earhart defended women's role in aviation at a *New York Herald Tribune* forum, "Women and the Changing World," at the Waldorf-Astoria Hotel in New York City. Eleanor Roosevelt opened the program, and President Roosevelt closed it by means of a radio broadcast. In her speech, Earhart concentrated on the lack of opportunities for women in aviation and the unfair wages received by the few who could get jobs. She advocated that women be treated as the equals of men.

In the audience was Dr. Edward Elliott, president of Purdue University. He was so impressed with Earhart's talk that he offered her a part-time job counseling the women students at Purdue on careers and advising Purdue's School of Aeronautics. Earhart accepted. Because her lecture schedule for the rest of 1934 was heavily booked, she would begin her work at Purdue in the fall semester of 1935. When Dr. Elliott announced her appointment, he said:

After she and Putnam moved to North Hollywood, Earhart would frequently associate with movie stars such as Douglas Fairbanks (left) and Fay Wray (right).

Miss Earhart represents better than any other young woman of this generation the spirit and the courageous skill of what may be called the new pioneering. At no point in our educational system is there greater need for pioneering and constructive planning than in education for women. The University believes Amelia Earhart will help us to see and to attack successfully many unsolved problems.[77]

The Move to California

In October 1934 Earhart flew to California to get some rest. Her vacation ended abruptly on November 3 when Putnam called to tell her that the house at Rye had burned. Many of her papers were lost in the fire, as well as their Rockwell Kent paintings and one wing of the house. Her medals and other awards were safe in the box in which she had stored them.

After the fire they decided to live in North Hollywood. Earhart had always loved California, and Putnam would be near his work at Paramount Pictures. In Hollywood Earhart and Putnam associated with a roster of movie stars—Mary Pickford, Douglas Fairbanks, William Hart, Will Rogers, and Gary Cooper. Earhart became friendly with another pilot, Jacqueline Cochran, and her husband, millionaire Floyd Odlum.

The reporters in California kept pestering Earhart about rumors of another record-setting flight that she was planning. Publicly she denied having any such plan. Privately she was outlining in detail a flight she had been considering for some

Putnam and Earhart are greeted by a Hawaiian child in Honolulu before her flight from Hawaii to California. The flight generated much bad publicity for Earhart as reporters criticized her for flying for purely commercial reasons.

time. No pilot had ever flown solo from Honolulu to the U.S. mainland—twenty-four hundred miles. Ten had died trying. She would be the first to make it. She asked Paul Mantz, an experienced pilot, to be her technical adviser. Since Amy Earhart was visiting her daughter and George Putnam in North Hollywood then, Earhart for the first time told her mother in advance of her flight plans.

On December 22, 1934, Earhart, Putnam, Mantz, and his wife, Myrtle, sailed for Honolulu with Earhart's Vega tied to the ship's deck. When they landed, Earhart told reporters that she had brought her plane so that they could fly from island to island. The reporters did not believe her.

The Honolulu and Mexican Flights

The reporters condemned this flight from Hawaii to California, which they called a stunt. She would prove nothing. Then the reporters learned that Putnam had persuaded the Hawaiian Sugar Planters Association to sponsor her flight with a ten-thousand-dollar prize for her if she made it to California. The vigor of the newspapers' antagonism scared the sugar planters into withdrawing their support. An angry Earhart confronted their committee. After accusing them of cowardice, she told them that she would make the flight—with or without their support. They reinstated the ten thousand dollars.

On January 11, 1935, Earhart took off from Honolulu. During the flight she talked with Putnam on the radio, which was the first two-way radio to be installed in a civilian plane: "I heard my husband's voice as if he were in the next room saying, 'AE, the noise of your motor interferes with your broadcast. Will you please try to speak a little louder so we can hear you!'"[78] The Vega functioned well all the way. About eighteen hours after she had left Honolulu, Earhart announced on her radio that she was on course and would land at Oakland, California, in a few minutes. Between five and ten thousand fans were there to greet her. She landed with two new world records: first person to fly solo over the Pacific and first person to fly solo over both the Atlantic and the Pacific.

Mexico City–to–Newark Flight

In Soaring Wings *Putnam defends Earhart's flight from Mexico City to Newark, New Jersey, with quotations from a newspaper:*

"The *Christian Science Monitor* said, 'Not for a record. . . . Not for the clamor of the crowd. . . . Nor for money, nor for science, not for "posterity," not for anything but the fact that she is that kind of girl, and that kind of flier, and likes that kind of fidelity to personal aspiration.

Paul Collins, with more than 1,000,000 miles of his own in the air, watched Miss Earhart's riding lights as she swung over the field, shook his head slowly with admiration, smiled slightly, said softly, 'That's a flier!'

And Doctor Kimball—"Doc Kimball the weather man" the fliers call him with affection—said, "Such people are good for us all."' "

Earhart with her mother in California, where Earhart and Putnam were living in 1935

The Honolulu flight refueled her popularity. In the spring New York University students voted that the two best-known men in the world were President Roosevelt and Adolf Hitler; the two best-known women, Eleanor Roosevelt and Amelia Earhart. Again taking advantage of her celebrity, Putnam, who had resigned from Paramount and was now her full-time manager, easily filled her lecture tour. He had scheduled her first speech within just a few days, so that without any real rest, she resumed her lectures.

After ending her tour in the Midwest, Earhart met the consul general of Mexico, who invited her to fly to Mexico. She told Putnam, "It's the first time I've been asked anywhere. I just *went* to Ireland."[79] To finance the flight, Putnam was able to persuade the Mexican government to print a postage stamp commemorating her visit. Putnam bought three hundred of the stamps, enclosed them in cases

Earhart is greeted by Eduardo Willsenon, consul general of Mexico, after her Mexico flight. Putnam again sparked controversy for Earhart when he used the Mexico flight to make money by printing postage stamps that commemorated the flight.

autographed by Earhart, and sold them to collectors. Some criticized his commercialism, but the stamps covered the cost of her flight. On April 20, 1935, Earhart flew her Vega from Burbank, California, to Mexico City in thirteen hours and thirty-two minutes—another record.

After Earhart and Putnam had spent two weeks touring Mexico, she took off on May 8 and flew to Newark, New Jersey— 2,125 miles. Wiley Post, a Lockheed test pilot, had warned her not to make that flight because flying over the Gulf of Mex-

ico was too dangerous. The flight turned out to be one of her easiest. As she was flying over the gulf in daylight, she realized that since her previous ocean flights had been at night, she had not seen much of the ocean. "So, on that sunny morning out of sight of land, I promised my lovely red Vega I'd fly her across no more water. And I promised myself that any further over-ocean flying would be attempted in a plane with more than one motor, capable of keeping aloft with a single engine. Just in case."[80] Those promises she kept.

Chapter

7 Last Flight

For the next two years, while Earhart maintained her lecture schedule, she also kept her commitment to Dr. Elliott and Purdue University. She counseled women students about careers and lectured at the School of Aeronautics. When a group of Purdue alumni gave Earhart a two-engine Lockheed Electra monoplane, she decided to try for one last record—to fly around the world at the equator. Afterwards she would settle down to lecturing, counseling at Purdue, and flying for her own pleasure.

Counseling at Purdue

Earhart worked into her lecture schedule from 1935 to 1937 the career counseling sessions that she had promised Elliott. Although he wanted her to counsel women students about career choices, he also wanted her on campus as a role model. He invited Dr. Lillian Gilbreth, an engineer and time-management specialist, to Purdue for the same reasons. Helen Schleman, a counselor then but later dean of women, remembered both of them: "The choice of visiting role models could not have been better. They were world famous achievers in their own right—the real forerunners of the modern day women's movement."[81]

Earhart was at Purdue two or three days each month. Having a room in the women's dormitory, she sometimes left her door open so that students could go in freely to talk with her. During the evening meal in the dining room, Earhart ate with the students. After dinner they often stayed at the table to continue their talk with Earhart, who usually sat with her elbows on the table, her chin resting on her hands—much to the dismay of the dean of women, who was trying to enforce good manners. Usually a group followed Earhart to the dormitory counselor's room, where they all, including Earhart, sat on the floor and talked.

In her lectures and in her informal talks, Earhart encouraged the women students to pursue careers. They could be doctors, scientists, historians, engineers—whatever they wanted to be. Marriage could wait, or they could combine marriage and a career. When word of her advice circulated around campus, a men's senior honorary group asked to talk with her. They wanted to protest her suggestions to the girls. When she asked why, they answered, "It's hard enough to get the girls to marry us, as it is!"[82]

While she was at Purdue, Earhart conducted a survey among the women students. She asked them, "If you were the wage earner and your husband ran the home, would you consider his work financially equivalent to yours?"[83] Sixty-seven percent said they would. Earhart was disappointed, for she thought a career outside the home was more demanding.

Earhart enjoyed the counseling work at Purdue. She wrote her mother, "The work has been very interesting and has served to crystallize some of my ideas which were rather formless before."[84]

In the mid-1930s Earhart occasionally mentioned another long flight. At a dinner party at Purdue, Putnam casually alluded to a "Purdue flying laboratory" in front of Elliott. Eventually the Purdue Research Foundation gave eighty thousand dollars, donated by private benefactors, to Earhart to buy a plane. On March 20, 1936, she ordered her first two-engine monoplane, a powerful Lockheed Electra. Although she had some vague plans about doing research for Purdue's School of Aeronautics, she had a different project in mind first. She would try for another

record, this time flying around the world at the equator. Other pilots had flown around the world, but not at the equator.

Preparing for the Around-the-World Flight

Putnam would handle the business of the flight—ordering fuel and spare parts to be available at her planned stopovers, getting landing permits, asking the government to build a runway on the American-owned Howland Island in the central Pacific Ocean, and publicizing the flight. Captain Harry Manning of the SS *Roosevelt* had volunteered to be the navigator. Earhart again asked Paul Mantz to be her technical adviser.

While all of the preparations were being made, Earhart was still lecturing to make money for the flight. She was so busy that she neglected her mother even more than usual. To make up for her in-

Earhart's Electra is wheeled to its hangar. Earhart would use the plane in her attempt to fly around the world.

Earhart with Paul Mantz, her technical adviser for the around-the-world flight (left). Mantz equipped the Electra with state-of-the-art technology, especially the radio equipment that would be used to keep in contact with Earhart. Earhart tests the radio equipment on board the Electra (right). Western Electric furnished the equipment, including supplying a Morse code key that would transmit long distances. Earhart found the Morse system cumbersome.

difference, Earhart made reservations for Amy and cousin Nancy Balis for a three-week tour of Europe.

On July 21, 1936, Earhart flew the Electra for the first time. The next day the *Los Angeles Times* ran a cover story about Earhart and her flying laboratory. The article listed some of the equipment Mantz had installed: a robot pilot, a fuel minimizer, instruments for flying blind through storms, wind deicers, and radio homing and two-way radio instruments. Mantz had given particular attention to the radio equipment, because Earhart had liked the two-way radio that she had on the Vega on her Honolulu-to-Oakland flight.

Western Electric had furnished a radio transmitter and a four-band receiver, both with power adequate for her needs. Included was an emergency frequency that she could use with a Morse code transmitting key and trailing aerial, or antenna. Never comfortable with the Morse code telegraphy, she had not used it for several years and was not enthusiastic about using it on this trip. Although Mantz insisted that she might need it, she did not bother to review the Morse code. To use the trailing aerial, she would have to reel it out in order to reach the desired transmission distance. Earhart thought the aerial was cumbersome, and it was, but it would

Earhart at Purdue

Purdue University honored Earhart after her death by hanging her portrait on campus. In a speech given at the April 13, 1975, dedication ceremony Dean of Women Helen B. Schleman recalled Earhart's time on campus:

"It was after dinners that as many students as could would follow Miss Earhart into my room and sit around on the floor and talk and listen. I probably don't have to say that Miss Earhart sat on the floor, too—she was adaptable, easy, and informal. The conversations invariably centered around Miss Earhart's belief that women should have and really did have choices about what they could do with their lives. She believed that women could be engineers or scientists; they could be physicians as well as nurses. She believed in women's intelligence, their ability to learn and their ability to do whatever they wanted to do. She had the courage herself to try anything and she encouraged the women students to believe in themselves enough to try whatever interested them. She saw no reason for limitations on their aspirations. There was no question that she, through her own achievements and persuasiveness, was an effective catalyst to heretofore unthinkable thoughts for all of us."

increase the distance that she could transmit messages.

On her thirty-ninth birthday, July 24, 1936, Earhart officially accepted the plane from Purdue. Training for the twenty-seven-thousand-mile flight began immediately. She practiced flying by instruments only in Mantz's blind-flying trainer. Flying many hours, she familiarized herself with the Electra. Mantz taught her how to handle the two engines. At first she tried to compensate for the plane's swaying motion by jockeying the two engines—adjusting first one throttle, then the other. Mantz warned her never to do that because the plane would ground loop. Instead she should return to idle speed and start over.

Some of her colleagues, especially Louise Thaden and Jackie Cochran, tried to persuade Earhart not to make this flight. She had already proved herself as a pilot; she did not need another record. Earhart smiled and went ahead with her plans.

If anyone could have convinced her not to go, it would have been Cochran. Although they had met only three years earlier, they had become real friends. Earhart and Cochran were not rivals, for Cochran loved racing, and Earhart preferred long-range flying. Their friendship must have been based on the attraction of opposites. Earhart was a soft-spoken, educated gentlewoman. Cochran, born to poverty, had only a third-grade education. Petite and attractive, she could at times talk louder than any man, and when provoked, she could outswear them, too. With determined hard work, she had established a successful cosmetic firm, was wealthy in her own right, and had married a millionaire, Floyd Odlum. In 1936 and 1937, the Odlums' estate in Indio, California, was Earhart's retreat. She could go there even if the Odlums were away.

Cochran claimed that she knew Earhart better than anyone else in the world—better even than Putnam did. Because the basis of their friendship was flying, she was probably right. Sharing an interest in extrasensory perception (ESP), as well, they had tried several experiments together. Cochran had hunches, and her hunches about Earhart's proposed flight were negative. Earhart believed in hunches, too, but she still would not abandon her plans for the long flight. Cochran could understand her decision. "Although she [Cochran] flew for the love of it, she realized that her new friend was seeking in flight an elusive peace, one she had failed to find in college, nursing, social work, or any of her earlier pursuits," wrote biographer Doris Rich.[85]

Earhart had a difficult time justifying this flight and its enormous expense—in the middle of the Great Depression—to the media. She wanted one more record. Men had flown around the world, but no woman had. She would be the first woman, and she would do it the hard way. She would circle the world at its longest distance, around the equator, a route no other pilot had flown.

By January 1937 Earhart was absolutely committed to the planned flight, but she was not able to concentrate on just the flight. Hours that she should have spent getting experience in handling the Electra she spent supervising the building of the new home in which she and Putnam would live in Hollywood. She had included a room for her mother, so that Amy could live with them after the world flight. Earhart also interviewed and hired a staff for the new house—gardener, houseman, housekeeper, and secretary.

One of the secretary's immediate jobs was to help Earhart with her mail, which, as always, increased as the takeoff date for the

Earhart packs for her around-the-world flight. Earhart had little air time on the Electra before the flight.

new flight drew near. Many people, including several youths, volunteered to accompany her, as she described in *Last Flight:*

> To air-minded youth a jaunt around the equator appears pretty inviting. Judging from the messages, a staggering number of boys and girls stood ready to embark.
>
> "I am 15 years old, quiet and want to see the world. I have no money, but will work my head off."
>
> "Please teach me to fly. I will repay you if it takes the rest of my life. I haven't got much because my father loads coal in a mine."[86]

Meanwhile, in New York, Putnam was laying some of the advance groundwork for the flight. He and Earhart imposed on their friendship with the Roosevelts to get top priority service in securing landing permits and getting the help of the U.S. Navy, if needed. Earhart stepped up the pace of her lectures.

Financial backing for this flight was difficult to obtain, partly because ocean flights had lost their novelty. Seeking another way to pay for the flight, Putnam committed Earhart to writing a continuing description of the journey. She would send in an installment from each stopover to the *New York Herald Tribune.* He also found more product endorsements for her—Bausch and Lomb, Bendix, and Standard Oil. He scheduled seventy lectures for her after the flight's completion, and he negotiated a book contract with Harcourt Brace. He arranged with Gimbel's, a New York department store, to sponsor sixty-five hundred stamp covers like those sold in an earlier deal with Mexico. Earhart agreed to autograph and carry the stamp covers on the Electra and then sell them after her return.

Paul Mantz worried that Earhart was doing everything except the two things she needed most to do—fly the Electra until she could really control it and get

A Dissenter Speaks Against Earhart

Aviation columnist Al Williams was contemptuous of Earhart's "first flights," as shown in an excerpt quoted by Susan Ware in Still Missing:

"'[The] personal profit angle in dollars and cents, and the struggle for personal fame, have been carefully camouflaged and presented under the banner of "scientific progress,"' Williams claimed. He was especially critical of the thousands of dollars that Earhart and her 'manager-husband' would make on the stamp cachets, which belied the labeling of the flight as 'purely scientific' for public consumption. He ended by calling on the Bureau of Air Commerce not to grant 'Mr. and Mrs. Amelia Earhart' permission for their next 'out-of-the-cockpit and on-to-Broadway flights.'"

Mantz, Earhart, navigator Manning, and backup navigator Noonan pose for cameras before the around-the-world flight.

some much needed rest. Nonetheless, on February 12, 1937, Earhart—who had been so busy that she had forgotten her own wedding anniversary party on February 3—announced the proposed world flight at a news conference in New York City. Then Earhart, accompanied by Putnam, Manning, and Lockheed mechanic Bo McNeely, flew to Burbank, California.

Both Mantz and Cochran questioned whether Manning could do the high-speed aerial navigation, which was far different from the slower ocean navigation. Four days before flight takeoff, Earhart heeded their advice and hired a backup navigator. Captain Fred Noonan had been a highly skilled navigator-pilot for Pan American Airways until the company fired him for being an alcoholic. Desperate to find work, Noonan promised Earhart that he would not drink on the flight.

Instruments and details were checked and rechecked. When Paul Mantz finally pronounced the plane ready for flight, Earhart flew the Electra to Oakland, with Putnam, Mantz, Manning, and Noonan on board. Unfortunately, rainy weather day after day had turned the unpaved Oakland Airport runway into mud.

On March 17, 1937, the runway was finally dry enough to support Earhart's Electra. Since several of the reporters had become bored by the repeated delays, only a few were at the airport when she finally lifted the plane into the air. One *San Francisco Chronicle* photographer managed to take a dramatic photograph of the Electra crossing above the Golden Gate Bridge on its way to Honolulu, the first stop on her flight. On board were Manning and Noonan, as well as Mantz, who was hitching a ride to Hawaii.

The crew landed at Wheeler Field in Honolulu fifteen hours and fifty-two minutes later, a record for an east-to-west crossing. When a storm delayed the takeoff for Howland Island the next day, friends invited the crew to a luau. However, as biographer Jean Backus tells, a pensive and tired "Amelia walked away from the party, striding far down the beach beneath Diamond Head, a slim and

(Left) Earhart flies over San Francisco Bay and (right) emerges from her plane after crashing in Honolulu. Although Earhart would maintain that the crash was not her fault, both Mantz and Manning disagreed.

lonely figure in the same brown slacks and leather jacket she had worn from Oakland. She was nearly forty years old and looked younger."[87]

A Costly Mistake

After the storm had abated, on March 20 Earhart, Manning, and Noonan sped down the Luke Field runway in preparation for taking off, when the plane suddenly ground looped. Although Earhart avoided an explosion by turning off the engine immediately, one wing and the underside of the plane, including the landing gear, were badly damaged. When Earhart climbed out of the plane, she said only, "Something must have gone wrong."[88]

Later she was more specific: "Witnesses said the tire blew. However, studying the tracks carefully, I believe that may not have been the primary cause of the accident. Possibly the landing gear's right shock absorber, as it lengthened, may have given way."[89] Mantz was convinced—and Manning later confirmed—that Earhart had done precisely what he had told her repeatedly never to do: She had jockeyed the throttles.

The plane would have to go back to California for extensive and expensive repairs. Such a beginning would have discouraged many pilots from continuing the flight, but when someone asked Earhart if she would try again, she answered without hesitation, "Of course."[90]

Back to California

On the ship sailing back to California, Earhart considered her situation. Her pride had answered "of course." After the shock had abated, her common sense began to reckon the cost. Repairs would total at least twenty-five thousand dollars. Rescheduling the stopovers would total another twenty-five thousand dollars. Putnam thought that he could raise at least twenty thousand dollars. Floyd Odlum gave another ten thousand dollars. Vincent Bendix, who had already helped with the first flight, contributed another twenty thousand dollars. Richard Byrd returned the fifteen hundred dollars that Earhart had given his expedition. Bernard Baruch, businessman and statesman, sent twenty-five hundred dollars, "Because I like your everlasting guts!"[91] To publicize the need for contributions, Earhart appeared on a radio program, the *Kraft Music Hour*, with singer Bing Crosby, Putnam, and Mantz. She spent a day at Gimbel's to spur the sale of another thousand of the stamp covers. The mechanics at Lockheed worked on a Sunday without pay to help her. The plane was repaired.

Second Attempt

Plans for the second attempt underwent some changes. His leave almost over, Manning returned to his ship. Noonan would be both navigator and backup pilot. Global weather changes forced them to fly from west to east this time. Putnam would fly with her and Noonan to Miami; then she and Noonan would take off from there.

Paul Mantz was in St. Louis on the day that Earhart, Noonan, and Putnam flew to Miami. She had not notified him that she would leave from there. Because he thought that Putnam was pushing her too hard, Mantz was convinced that she was too tired to begin such a grueling trip. Besides, he had planned to work more on the radio with Earhart. He suspected that he had been left behind because Putnam wanted her to get going without any further delay.

On June 1, 1937, at 5:56 A.M., Earhart and Noonan took off from Miami on what was to be her last big flight. Not seeing any need for the Morse code transmitter key or the trailing antenna, she had deliberately left them in Miami. After all, she had not needed them on any of her previous flights.

Earhart and Noonan were to fly by day and stop each night at a scheduled place for refueling and maintenance. Their route would take them from Miami to Puerto Rico, Venezuela, Dutch Guiana,

After her plane was repaired, Earhart appointed Fred Noonan (left of Earhart) as both her navigator and backup pilot.

Brazil, Africa, Pakistan, India, Singapore, Java, Australia, Lae in New Guinea, Howland Island, Hawaii, and California.

Wherever they stopped along the way, fuel was waiting for them in huge drums with "Amelia Earhart" painted on the sides. Spare plane parts were also available. If the plane needed only a routine servicing, they were on their way the next morning. If the plane needed major repairs, they stayed two or three days, with the chance to see a little of the country and its people. Earhart described their stopovers in *Last Flight:*

> The geography of our journey likely will remain most clearly memorized in terms of landing-field environments; of odors of baking metal, gasoline and perspiring ground crews; of the roar of warming motors and the clatter of metal-working tools. Such impressions competed with the lovely sights of the

Earhart and Noonan have lunch with airport employees after landing at the second stop of their around-the-world flight, Caripito, Venezuela.

Earhart and Noonan pose for the cameras and show the route of their flight.

new worlds we glimpsed: the delectable perfumes of flowers, spices and fragrant countryside; the sounds and songs and music of diverse peoples.[92]

Usually the guests of some local official, Earhart and Noonan only occasionally stayed in a hotel. Always, however, they were welcomed with a banquet, even if it was served in a hangar.

In several places Earhart would have liked to stay longer, as she wrote in the daily log:

> *Push through.* I find myself writing those words almost resentfully. We're always pushing through, hurrying on our long way, trying to get some other place instead of enjoying the place we'd already got to. A situation, alas, about which there is no use complaining. After all, this was not a voyage of sight-seeing.[93]

Twenty Thousand Miles Flown, Seven Thousand Yet to Fly

When they arrived at Lae, New Guinea, on June 29, they had been traveling for nearly a month and had covered twenty thousand miles. They had flown through monsoon rains, sandstorms, heat waves, rainstorms, and strong air currents—all without a major crisis. The excessive heat in the plane's cockpit was a constant aggravation, however.

In talking with Putnam from India, Earhart told him that she was having "personnel trouble." Biographer Rich reports that according to Paul Collins and Gene Vidal, Putnam told Earhart to cancel the rest of the trip. She replied that "'there was only one stop left and I'm pretty sure I can handle the situation.' GP did not explain what Amelia had meant by 'person-

nel trouble,' but Collins and Vidal assumed that Noonan was drinking."[94]

Earhart had hoped to take off from Lae by June 31 because Putnam had scheduled her to speak at a Fourth of July celebration in Oakland. When Noonan learned that bad weather and repairs would keep them in Lae for two or three extra days, he settled in for a night's drinking.

Earhart and Noonan spent one day repacking the Electra. They discarded every nonessential item. They had already shipped home the parachutes because they would be useless over the Pacific.

In one of her articles for the *New York Herald Tribune*, Earhart wrote:

> Not much more than a month ago I was on the other shore of the Pacific, looking westward. This evening, I look eastward over the Pacific. In those fast-moving days which have intervened, the whole width of the world has

In a publicity photo, Earhart checks the plane's gas tanks during a stopover.

passed behind us—except for this broad ocean. I shall be glad when we have left the hazards of its navigation behind us.[95]

When they finally prepared to take off from Lae, both Earhart and Noonan were near exhaustion. Along the way Earhart had occasionally suffered from dysentery and was sometimes nauseated from the gas fumes. Noonan's substitution of alcohol for food had taken its toll of him, too. Pictures of them at Lae showed underweight people with tired, strained faces. Biographer Doris Rich summarized Earhart's problems:

Taking precedence was her own exhaustion. On some days she had flown over 1000 miles. Since Miami she had flown on twenty-one of thirty days, on three of those days for more than thirteen hours, and another seven of them, for more than seven hours. Her previous long-distance flights had been a matter of hours, not weeks. She was never physically strong, only determined.[96]

The Takeoff for Howland Island

On Friday, July 2, at 10:00 A.M. (July 1, 12:30 P.M., Howland time), they started down the thousand-foot dirt runway weighed down with just over a thousand gallons of fuel. They were going to fly 2,556 miles over an ocean with few landmarks to find Howland Island, a pinpoint of land barely a mile and a half long. Earhart had calculated that the flight would take about 18.5 hours.

The Coast Guard cutter *Itasca*, captained by Commander W. K. Thompson, had been dispatched to stand by Howland Island to lead the Electra to the island by radio communication. Commander Thom-

It Helps to Know the President

Earhart needed the Works Project Administration (WPA) to build a runway on Howland Island. She appealed to President Roosevelt for help in a letter quoted by Mary Lovell in The Sound of Wings:

"Am now informed apparently some question regarding WPA appropriation in amount of three thousand dollars which covers all costs other than those borne by me for this mid Pacific pioneer landing field which permanently useful and valuable aeronautically and nationally. Requisition now on desk of A.V. Keene, Bureau of Budget, Treasury Department. Understand its moving requires executive approval under circumstances could you expedite as immediate action vital . . . please forgive troublesome female flyer for whom the Howland Island project is key to world flight attempt?"

In the last known photo taken of Earhart and Noonan, the two pose with a gold miner in Lae, New Guinea.

pson did not know that Earhart had left the homing aerial and the Morse code transmitter key in Miami. On board the *Itasca* was Putnam's representative, Richard Black, of the Department of the Interior, who was giving Thompson confusing, sometimes contradictory, information. That Earhart and Noonan would cross two time zones and the international date line further compounded the confusion. Thompson finally decided to wait until he heard from Earhart herself.

He had to wait until 2:45 A.M., July 2, Howland time, when the radio operator finally heard her voice. She came on again at 3:45, and this time they heard her say, "Earhart. Overcast. Will listen on 3105 kilocycles on hour and half hour."[97] She came on at intervals and asked for the ship's position. Because she had left part of the communication equipment in Miami, she could not hear their responses. And she did not stay on the air long enough for them to take a bearing on her

position. The *Itasca* sent up heavy black smoke that would be visible for twenty miles. Sometimes her message was garbled; sometimes she whistled, but not long enough to take a bearing; sometimes she was transmitting on the wrong frequency. She came on at 6:45, 7:42, and again at 8:00. They could hear her, but she could not hear them, although the ship's radio operator was sending on every possible frequency. According to biographer Rich, "At 8:44 Amelia's voice— shrill and breathless, her words tumbling over one another—came in. 'We are on the line of position 156-137. We are running north and south.'"[98] She did not broadcast again.

The Search Began

Historian Susan Ware, in *Still Missing*, describes the search that ensued:

Putnam and Noonan's wife look over reports on their missing spouses. Earhart and Noonan were never found, and what happened to the two remains a mystery.

Within an hour the captain of the *Itasca* had concluded that they were out of fuel (they had been in the air for almost twenty-four hours at that point) and began a search. The search lasted for a week, at a cost of four mil-lion dollars. Despite covering approximately 250,000 miles at sea, the most extensive air and sea search in U.S. history found no trace of the fliers or their plane.[99]

Putnam pursued every lead. He even asked Jackie Cochran to try ESP. She did and believed that Earhart had lived for two days. Then the images stopped, and she concluded that Earhart had died. Muriel accepted the theory that Amelia had gone down with her plane, but Amy never did fully believe that Amelia was dead.

The Search Continues

Rumors and hoaxes have surfaced occasionally since Earhart's disappearance. In addition several people, convinced that they can find Earhart's grave or some identifying piece of evidence, mounted and are continuing to mount search parties to some of the Pacific islands. They have found pieces of metal from planes, a navigator's box, the sole of a woman's shoe, a blindfold, bones in shallow graves. So far, however, no indisputable proof has been discovered to link any of those objects to Earhart. Amelia Earhart is still missing.

She Was Her Own Best Example

Amelia Earhart was important as an airplane pilot, as a feminist, and as a role model. In several of her endeavors, especially flying planes and promoting women's rights, she was ahead of her time in her thinking. Her fame has endured partially because she disappeared mysteriously, but also because she was a remarkable woman.

Earhart's Importance in Aviation

Earhart straddled two eras in aviation. When she learned to fly, both she and aviation were young. Early pilots, who needed no license, vied for speed and altitude records and flew in air shows, where they did stunts and took fans for rides. Even back then Earhart foresaw the day when planes would be bigger, faster, more powerful. Muriel recalled Amelia's describing planes of the future: "She said that some day we would have airplanes large enough to carry ten or a dozen passengers, and they'd go on regular schedules like trains. She envisioned flights across the country and around the world."[100]

Earhart's foresight proved accurate a few years later when she stepped into the next age of aviation, commercial air passenger service. Her role in commercial aviation was on the secondary level of management, however, not on the primary level of piloting. Because Earhart was such a persuasive saleswoman, she was always

Earhart tirelessly worked to increase the popularity of flying and to make young women aware that their options went beyond the home. She is remembered now as she hoped to be remembered—a pioneer.

Women's Place in Aviation

Historian Susan Ware, in Still Missing, *quotes Earhart to suggest the importance of every flight made by a woman:*

"If women proved themselves, opportunities would expand and prejudice would recede. 'Each accomplishment, no matter how small, is important,' Earhart told fellow pilot Louise Thaden. 'Although it may be no direct contribution to the science of aeronautics nor to its technical development, it will encourage other women to fly. The more women who fly, the more who become pilots, the quicker we will be recognized as an important factor in aviation.' The course of aviation did not prove to be so simple, but that did not keep women like Amelia Earhart from trying—and flying."

the vice president of public relations. She wrote and lectured about the convenience, comfort, and safety of air travel.

While Earhart was promoting air passenger service, she was also pursuing her own ambition in aviation—to be the first to fly uncharted air routes. All but one of her record-breaking flights were made in a small, single-engine plane. Daring, courage, determination, single-mindedness—these traits were both the cornerstone of her piloting and the basis for her appeal to the public.

Although Earhart was the best-known woman pilot of her day, she was not the best woman pilot. She flew by the book, and if the book did not cover the situation, she often made poor judgments. Yet Earhart achieved some remarkable records, perhaps even more remarkable because she had only average flying skills. Her highest personal achievement was being the first woman to fly the Atlantic solo.

Earhart advanced the position of women in aviation by proving that women could fly and by supporting other women pilots in such projects as the Women's Air Derby. She usually listed as a reason for making a particular record flight that it was to prove what a woman could do. She was her own best example.

Even today Earhart commands admiration and respect. She really believed the advice she had given the women students at Purdue University: that they could take charge of their lives and become whatever they wanted to be. Earhart once observed, "Everyone has her own Atlantic to fly. Whatever you want very much to do, against the opposition of tradition, neighborhood opinion, and so-called common sense—that is an Atlantic."[101]

Another of Earhart's guiding principles has lasting importance. If people fail to fly their Atlantics, they should try again. In her lectures, and especially in talking to young people, she stressed achieving one's goal. She fulfilled her goals and lived her dreams in flying.

Earhart's Importance as a Feminist

As with aviation, so did Earhart straddle two eras in feminism. The feminists in the mid- and late-nineteenth century had been militants who banded together to fight discrimination against them in labor unions. Then in the early twentieth century individuals were more active than groups were. They did not regroup until after World War II. Earhart was one of the individuals between the two groups.

Earhart lectures in Hawaii. In her lectures, Earhart emphasized that everyone should attempt to accomplish their goals, no matter how farfetched or unconventional they may seem.

As in aviation, Earhart was her own best example of practicing her feminist beliefs. She urged women to have careers, as she did. She advised them to combine careers and marriage if they wanted both, as she did. Susan Ware, in *Still Missing*, quotes one of Earhart's views on marriage: "Why should marriage be a cyclone cellar into which a woman retreats from failures in the other sphere?"[102] Furthermore, marriage should not be a master-slave relationship, but an equal partnership, as hers was.

Earhart's modest, gracious manner did not diminish her determination to change the wrongs she saw in women's lot. Susan Ware summed up Earhart's position on feminism: "She knew who she was and what she wanted to do: preach the cause of aviation to the general public, and preach the cause of feminism to women."[103]

Earhart's Importance as a Role Model

Although young people were particularly devoted to Earhart, women of all ages were fans, too. A woman who heard Earhart speak to the Vermont legislature wrote to Earhart's mother, "We all thought Lindbergh was a marvel, but our 'Amelia' has shown the world what a woman can do." As biographer Doris Rich points out, "The writer, like most women of the time, could identify with a woman who combined the stuff of dreams with the demands of reality."[104]

At Purdue University Earhart was actually hired as a role model. Helen Schleman, a counselor who worked with Earhart, described her:

She had the courage herself to try anything and she encouraged the women students to believe in themselves enough to try whatever interested them. She saw no reason for limitations on their aspirations. There was no question that she, through her own achievements and persuasiveness, was an effective catalyst to heretofore unthinkable thoughts for all of us.[105]

Earhart especially wanted to reach young people. On a speaking engagement in Spokane, Washington, Earhart asked to talk with the high school girls in Girl Reserves, a group sponsored by the YWCA. In this unscheduled, unpaid appearance, Earhart talked casually with the girls about "Girl Reserves, life, being a person, and living according to one's ideal," as remembered by Edein French, one of the audience. French also recalled that she left the meeting "deeply influenced by [Earhart's] presence and determined to try to become a person like her."[106]

Young People Admired Earhart

In 1935 in Port Huron, Michigan, the winner of an essay contest would get to meet Earhart at a local air show. Susan Ware, in Still Missing, *would have chosen this essay by Francetta Cole, age thirteen:*

"In these days of progress Miss Earhart leads the way for women who wish to lead freer and wider lives. She is an inspiration to young women who, rather than stay home in the kitchen, would fly the air as birds. One hundred years ago our great-grandmothers had to keep their wings clipped like discontented little birds. A few ugly ducklings flew from the barnyard to become beautiful white swans. Amelia Earhart, as one of these, led the way so that others might dare follow. We, the women of America, feel grateful that she has shown us a way to make life a more interesting adventure."

Earhart speaks to students at her alma mater, Hyde Park High School, in 1928. Earhart always felt that encouraging young people was an important task.

Earhart receives an award for her accomplishments from President Herbert Hoover.

That episode and others like it imply that Earhart was consciously and conscientiously being a role model. Susan Ware, in *Still Missing*, agrees: "The entire record of her public career suggests that she used her own example as a model for other women to emulate." To expand her point, Ware adds, "One suspects that acting as a conscious role model was quite deliberate. It was also the essence of liberal feminism."[107]

Assessment

Evaluating the worth of someone's life is a task for a wise person like Walter Lippmann, American journalist and essayist who had a gift for stripping away pretensions to reveal the truth underneath. Six days after her disappearance, Lippmann wrote the following judgment of Amelia Earhart, as quoted by Putnam in *Soaring Wings:*

> I cannot quite remember whether Miss Earhart undertook her flight with some practical purpose in mind, say, to demonstrate something or other

about aviation which will make it a little easier for commercial passengers to move more quickly around the world. There are those who seem to think that an enterprise like hers must have some such justification.

But the world is a better place to live in because it contains human beings who will give up ease and security to do what they themselves think worth doing.

The best things of mankind are as useless as Amelia Earhart's adventure. In such persons mankind overcomes the inertia which would keep it earthbound forever in its habitual ways. They have in them the free and useless energy with which alone men surpass themselves.

Such energy cannot be planned and managed and made purposeful. It is wild and free. But all the heroes, the saints and the seers, the explorers and creators partake of it. They do the useless, brave, noble, the divinely foolish and the very wisest things that are done by man.[108]

Notes

Introduction: The Trailblazer

1.   Quoted in Doris L. Rich, *Amelia Earhart: A Biography*. Washington, DC: Smithsonian Institution, 1989.

Chapter 1: Earhart's Widespread, but Shallow, Roots

2.   Amelia Earhart, *The Fun of It*. 1932. Reprinted Chicago: Academy Chicago, 1977.

3.   Earhart, *The Fun of It*.

4.   Muriel Earhart Morrissey and Carol L. Osborne, *Amelia, My Courageous Sister*. Santa Clara, CA: Osborne, 1987.

5.   Morrissey and Osborne, *Amelia*.

6.   Jean L. Backus, *Letters from Amelia, 1901–1937*. Boston: Beacon Press, 1982.

7.   Earhart, *The Fun of It*.

8.   Earhart, *The Fun of It*.

9.   Morrissey and Osborne, *Amelia*.

10.   Earhart, *The Fun of It*.

11.   Quoted in Morrissey and Osborne, *Amelia*.

Chapter 2: Earhart Searches for Her Niche

12.   Earhart, *The Fun of It*.

13.   Earhart, *The Fun of It*.

14.   Earhart, *The Fun of It*.

15.   Amelia Earhart, *20 Hrs. 40 Mins.: Our Flight in the* Friendship. 1928. Reprinted New York: Arno Press, 1980.

16.   Earhart, *The Fun of It*.

17.   Quoted in Morrissey and Osborne, *Amelia*.

18.   Morrissey and Osborne, *Amelia*.

Chapter 3: The Friendship Flight

19.   Earhart, *20 Hrs. 40 Mins.*

20.   Quoted in Morrissey and Osborne, *Amelia*.

21.   Quoted in Morrissey and Osborne, *Amelia*.

22.   Quoted in Morrissey and Osborne, *Amelia*.

23.   Earhart, *The Fun of It*.

24.   Quoted in Mary S. Lovell, *The Sound of Wings: The Life of Amelia Earhart*. New York: St. Martin's Press, 1989.

25.   Earhart, *The Fun of It*.

26.   Quoted in John Burke, *Winged Legend: The Story of Amelia Earhart*. New York: Ballantine, 1970.

27.   Quoted in Rich, *Amelia Earhart*.

28.   Earhart, *20 Hrs. 40 Mins.*

Chapter 4: Changing Directions

29.   Quoted in Backus, *Letters from Amelia*.

30.   Quoted in Earhart, *The Fun of It*.

31.   Earhart, *20 Hrs. 40 Mins.*

32.   Earhart, *The Fun of It*.

33.   Earhart, *The Fun of It*.

34.   Earhart, *The Fun of It*.

35.   Earhart, *The Fun of It*.

36.   Earhart, *The Fun of It*.

37.   George Palmer Putnam, *Soaring Wings: A Biography of Amelia Earhart*. New York: Harcourt Brace, 1939.

38.   Quoted in Morrissey and Osborne, *Amelia*.

39.   Earhart, *The Fun of It*.

40.   Rich, *Amelia Earhart*.

41.   Rich, *Amelia Earhart*.

42.   Rich, *Amelia Earhart*.

43.   Quoted in Backus, *Letters from Amelia*.

44.   Quoted in Morrissey and Osborne, *Amelia*.

45.   Quoted in Putnam, *Soaring Wings*.

46.   Quoted in Morrissey and Osborne, *Amelia*.

47.   Quoted in Backus, *Letters from Amelia*.

Chapter 5: The Marriage Cage

48.   Quoted in Backus, *Letters from Amelia*.

49.   Earhart, *The Fun of It*.

50.   Earhart, *The Fun of It*.

51. Quoted in Backus, *Letters from Amelia.*

52. Quoted in Backus, *Letters from Amelia.*

53. Quoted in Backus, *Letters from Amelia.*

54. *The American Experience,* "Amelia Earhart." Nancy Porter Productions for PBS station WGBH, Boston, 1993. Television documentary.

55. Quoted in Backus, *Letters from Amelia.*

56. Quoted in Morrissey and Osborne, *Amelia.*

57. Quoted in Backus, *Letters from Amelia.*

58. Lovell, *The Sound of Wings.*

59. Quoted in Putnam, *Soaring Wings.*

60. Putnam, *Soaring Wings.*

61. Quoted in Backus, *Letters from Amelia.*

62. Backus, *Letters from Amelia.*

Chapter 6: Having to Be First

63. Putnam, *Soaring Wings.*

64. Earhart, *The Fun of It.*

65. Quoted in Putnam, *Soaring Wings.*

66. Quoted in Rich, *Amelia Earhart.*

67. Quoted in Rich, *Amelia Earhart.*

68. Earhart, *The Fun of It.*

69. Earhart, *The Fun of It.*

70. Quoted in Morrissey and Osborne, *Amelia.*

71. Quoted in Backus, *Letters from Amelia.*

72. Quoted in Backus, *Letters from Amelia.*

73. Quoted in Lovell, *The Sound of Wings.*

74. Quoted in Lovell, *The Sound of Wings.*

75. Quoted in Susan Ware, *Still Missing: Amelia Earhart and the Search for Modern Feminism.* New York: W. W. Norton, 1993.

76. Quoted in Ware, *Still Missing.*

77. Quoted in Putnam, *Soaring Wings.*

78. Amelia Earhart, *Last Flight.* 1937. Reprinted, New York: Crown, 1988.

79. Quoted in Lovell, *The Sound of Wings.*

80. Quoted in Vincent V. Loomis with Jeffrey L. Ethell, *Amelia Earhart: The Final Story.* New York: Random House, 1985.

Chapter 7: Last Flight

81. Helen B. Schleman, "Personal Recollections," speech delivered at dedication of the Amelia Earhart portrait at Earhart Hall, Purdue University, April 13, 1975.

82. Quoted in Schleman, "Personal Recollections."

83. "Views on Value of Household Work Show Little Change in Six Decades," Bloomington, Indiana, *Herald-Times,* January 24, 1993.

84. Quoted in Ware, *Still Missing.*

85. Rich, *Amelia Earhart.*

86. Earhart, *Last Flight.*

87. Backus, *Letters from Amelia.*

88. Quoted in Lovell, *The Sound of Wings.*

89. Earhart, *Last Flight.*

90. Quoted in Putnam, *Soaring Wings.*

91. Quoted in Morrissey and Osborne, *Amelia.*

92. Earhart, *Last Flight.*

93. Earhart, *Last Flight.*

94. Quoted in Rich, *Amelia Earhart.*

95. Earhart, *Last Flight.*

96. Rich, *Amelia Earhart.*

97. Quoted in Rich, *Amelia Earhart.*

98. Quoted in Rich, *Amelia Earhart.*

99. Ware, *Still Missing.*

Epilogue: She Was Her Own Best Example

100. Morrissey and Osborne, *Amelia.*

101. Quoted in Nancy Landon Kassebaum, "Letter to Irene Natividad," *Women's Political Times,* September/October 1989.

102. Quoted in Ware, *Still Missing.*

103. Ware, *Still Missing.*

104. Quoted in Rich, *Amelia Earhart.*

105. Schleman, "Personal Recollections."

106. Quoted in Ware, *Still Missing.*

107. Ware, *Still Missing.*

108. Quoted in Putnam, *Soaring Wings.*

For Further Reading

T. C. Buddy Brennan, *Witness to the Execution: The Odyssey of Amelia Earhart.* Frederick, CO: Renaissance House, 1988. Presenting "believable circumstantial evidence," Brennan concludes that Earhart was executed by the Japanese at Saipan.

Thomas E. Devine with Richard M. Daley, *Eyewitness: The Amelia Earhart Incident.* Frederick, CO: Renaissance House, 1987. Devine claims to have seen Earhart's plane at Saipan in 1944. He reportedly saw U.S. Navy Secretary James Forrestal witness the burning of her plane. Natives led Devine to what they claimed was the site of Earhart's grave.

Shannon Garst, *Amelia Earhart: Heroine of the Skies.* New York: Julian Messner, 1947. Emphasizes Earhart's adventurous life and her achievements.

Fred Goerner, *The Search for Amelia Earhart.* Garden City, NY: Doubleday, 1966. Goerner advances the theory that President Franklin Roosevelt had sent Earhart on a spy mission for the United States and that she was to photograph Japanese installations on the Marshall Islands. A native of Saipan told Goerner that Earhart had died of dysentery and was buried there.

Jane Leder, *Amelia Earhart.* San Diego, CA: Greenhaven Press, 1989. Leder briefly summarizes Earhart's life. She concentrates on Earhart's last flight and explores first the government's search, then the searches by Thomas Devine, Fred Goerner, Joe Klass, and Vincent Loomis. Leder remains objective in her analyses.

Judy Lomax, *Women of the Air.* New York: Dodd, Mead, 1987. This book is a collection of brief biographies of ten to fifteen pages that describes the women aviation pioneers—from the balloonists through the fliers of planes to the astronauts.

Carol A. Pearce, *Amelia Earhart.* New York: Facts On File, 1988. Pearce sees mostly the good in Earhart and obviously admires her tremendously.

Works Consulted

Books

Jean L. Backus, *Letters from Amelia, 1901–1937*. Boston: Beacon Press, 1982. The letters are from Amelia to her mother. The author weaves in Earhart's biography. The letters show aspects of Earhart not usually revealed: She could be a real scold, for example.

Randall Brink, *Lost Star: The Search for Amelia Earhart*. New York: W. W. Norton, 1994. The author has read declassified files from World War II as they have been released by the government. He believes that for her final flight the government substituted a faster, more powerful plane with increased fuel capacity for her Electra; that she did fly a spy mission but was captured by the Japanese; that she and Noonan were taken to Saipan and then to Tokyo; and that they were held in a prisoner of war camp in Japan or China during World War II. This account answers some questions not addressed in other search reports.

John Burke, *Winged Legend: The Story of Amelia Earhart*. New York: Ballantine, 1970. This biography is written in a popular, lively style.

Amelia Earhart, *The Fun of It*. 1932. Reprinted, Chicago: Academy Chicago, 1977. Earhart discusses her childhood, her love of flying, some of her flights, and the people she knew.

Amelia Earhart, *Last Flight*. 1937. Reprinted, New York: Crown, 1988. Earhart kept a daily log of her last flight and, until her disappearance, had faithfully sent installments home in preparation for the book she planned to publish. After her disappearance, George Palmer Putnam finished writing the book.

Amelia Earhart, *20 Hrs. 40 Mins.: Our Flight in the* Friendship. 1928. Reprinted New York: Arno Press, 1980. Earhart's first book describes the Atlantic flight that made her world famous.

Anne Morrow Lindbergh, *Hour of Gold, Hour of Lead: Diaries and Letters*. New York: Harcourt Brace Jovanovich, 1973. Lindbergh remembers meeting Earhart for the first time and was surprised to find herself liking her.

Vincent V. Loomis with Jeffrey L. Ethell, *Amelia Earhart: The Final Story*. New York: Random House, 1985. After an almost twenty-year search, Loomis concludes that Earhart had not been a spy, but that she had become lost and was captured by the Japanese, who considered her a spy. She died in a prisoner of war camp at Saipan, Loomis believes.

Mary S. Lovell, *The Sound of Wings: The Life of Amelia Earhart*. New York: St. Martin's, 1989. This biography was carefully researched and written. Lovell paints one of the fuller portraits of Earhart.

Muriel Earhart Morrissey and Carol L. Osborne, *Amelia, My Courageous Sister*. Santa Clara, CA: Osborne, 1987. Morrissey obviously loved and admired her sister. This account provides some information about the family not found in other biographies.

George Palmer Putnam, *Soaring Wings: A Biography of Amelia Earhart.* New York: Harcourt Brace, 1939. Putnam writes as much of himself as of Amelia Earhart, his wife. Naturally, perhaps, his view is highly selective. He, too, includes information not found in other sources.

Doris L. Rich, *Amelia Earhart: A Biography.* Washington, DC: Smithsonian Institution, 1989. Rich has written a lively, well-researched account of Earhart's life. The author generally presents opposing views.

Susan Ware, *Still Missing: Amelia Earhart and the Search for Modern Feminism.* New York: W. W. Norton, 1993. Ware analyzes Earhart as a feminist and places her in the history of the feminist movement.

Correspondence

Nancy Landon Kassebaum, "Letter to Irene Natividad," *Women's Political Times,* September/October 1989. Kassebaum refers to a key part of Earhart's personal philosophy.

Newspapers and Magazines

Paul Briand Jr., "Was She on a Secret Mission?" *womenSports,* October 1974. This article is a one-page summary of the speculative reports that Earhart was held in Tokyo during World War II.

Pete Hamill, "The Cult of Amelia Earhart." *Ms.,* September 1976. Hamill relates the high points of Earhart's life and speculates on the chances of her being sent on a spying mission by President Franklin Roosevelt.

"Views on Value of Household Work Show Little Change in Six Decades," Bloomington, Indiana, *Herald-Times,* January 24, 1993.

Recording

"Amelia Earhart," a Mark 56 record, No. 746, produced by George Garabedian, 1977. On side one Muriel Earhart Morrissey talks about Amelia Earhart. On side two Earhart discusses the importance of women in aviation, and the March 14, 1937, dedication ceremony of a plaque honoring her is recorded.

Speeches

Helen B. Schleman, "Personal Recollections," speech delivered at dedication of the Amelia Earhart portrait at Earhart Hall, Purdue University, April 13, 1975. In telling anecdotes about Earhart when she was a career counselor at Purdue, Schleman emphasized Earhart as a role model.

Television

The American Experience, "Amelia Earhart." Nancy Porter Productions for PBS station WGBH, Boston, 1993. Documentary.

Index

Picture Credits

Cover photo: UPI/Bettmann

AP/Wide World, 18, 43, 62, 67, 70, 71, 73, 80, 81, 82, 90 (both), 92 (bottom), 93, 95, 96, 97

The Bettmann Archive, 10, 36, 46, 47, 100

Library of Congress, 11, 28, 37, 39, 42 (both), 99, 101

Ninety-Nines Library, 54

Radcliffe College, 9, 12, 14, 15, 16 (both), 17, 19, 20, 21, 22, 24, 26 (both), 30, 48, 52, 76

© Smithsonian Institution, 25, 32, 84, 85 (both), 89, 91, 92 (top)

UPI/Bettmann, 23, 39 (both), 41, 44, 49, 53, 56, 57, 58, 59, 60, 65, 75, 77 (both), 79, 87

About the Author

A native of Indiana, Eileen Morey has undergraduate degrees in nursing and secondary education and a graduate degree in library science, all from Indiana University. She has a second master's degree in literature from the Bread Loaf School of English, Middlebury College, in Vermont. After a brief career in nursing, she became a high school English teacher, then a high school librarian. An avid reader, she is also a novice photographer. She lives in southern Indiana.